THE A-B-C OF ÆSTHETICS

BY LEO STEIN

SOLIS PRESS : ENGLAND

OF RELATED INTEREST ALSO PUBLISHED BY SOLIS PRESS:

Leo Stein, *Appreciation: Painting, Poetry and Prose*
Roger Fry, *The Artist and Psycho-Analysis*
Henri Bergson, *Creative Evolution*
Henri Bergson, *Matter and Memory*

First published in 1927 by Boni & Liveright, USA.
This new edition published in 2024 by Solis Press.
There have been some minor changes and corrections.

Caution: please be aware that some of the language used
is of its time.

Title page: a facsimile of the first printing

Cover image: Paul Cézanne, *The Vase of Tulips*, 1885–95. The Mr. and
Mrs. Lewis Larned Coburn Memorial Collection, courtesy of the
Art Institute of Chicago.

ISBN: 978-1-910146-77-4 (paperback)

ISBN: 978-1-910146-78-1 (hardback)

Ebooks are available

~

Published by Solis Press, Lytchett House, 13 Freeland Park, Wareham Road,
Poole BH16 6FA, England

Contents

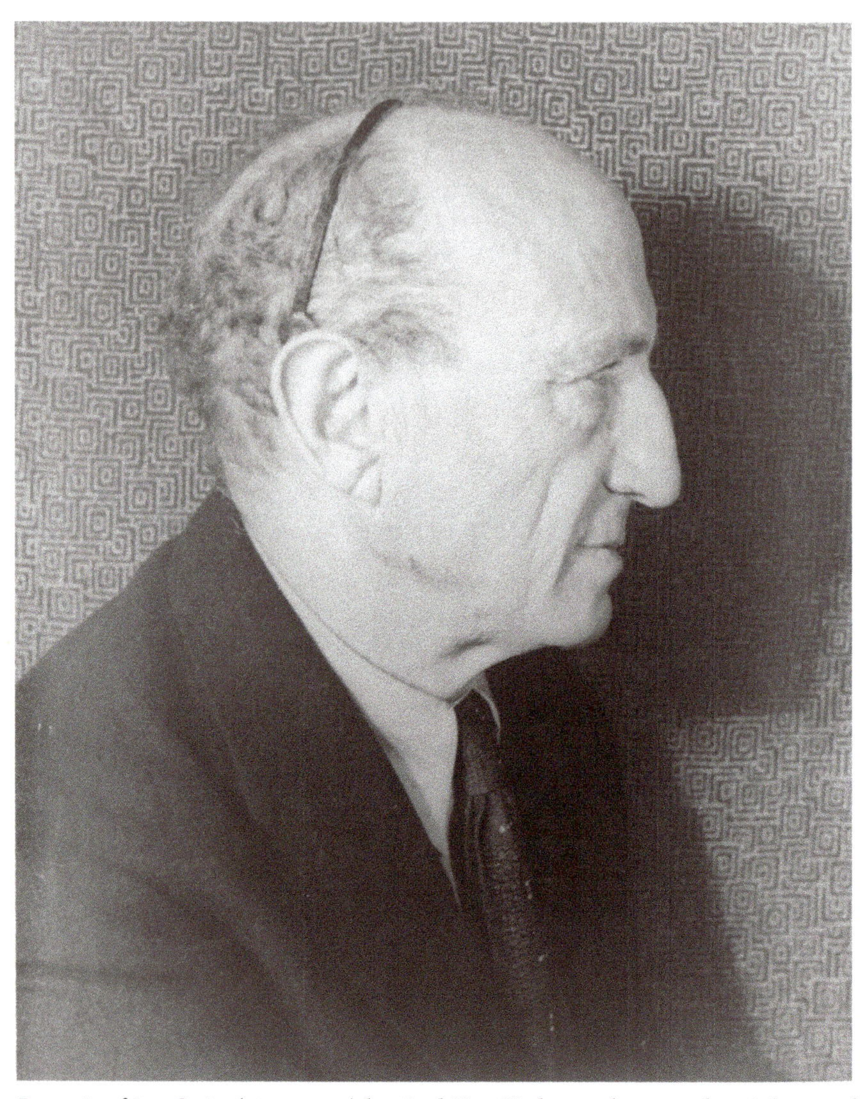

Portrait of Leo Stein (1872–1947) by Carl Van Vechten, photographer. Library of Congress Prints and Photographs Division Washington, D.C. 20540 USA.

Preface

I have called this book *The A-B-C of Aesthetics* for a somewhat unusual reason. An A-B-C book generally implies the existence of other more authoritative books upon the subject, to which it serves as an introduction. For aesthetics there are no such books. There are no authorities and it is somewhat doubtful whether the subject exists. Every fresh book on it is another attempt to put it on the map. By calling this little book *The A-B-C of Aesthetics* I mean to imply that it does not get very far but that it tries to start as near the beginning as possible. I have tried to write it clearly and simply, and I hope in that way also to have justified the title.

Leo Stein

I. On Being Intelligent

To be intelligent is simply, in any situation, to consider as part of that situation, anything that for the purposes in hand, belongs to that situation. To be unintelligent is to neglect something that belongs there, to fail in distinguishing that situation as the particular one that it actually is, to assume that the situation is satisfactorily understood when relevant facts have been ignored, facts which it would be possible and practicable to know. To be intelligent is to be perceptively open-minded.

Intelligence has nothing in especial to do with intellect. To be intelligent is not the same as to be intellectual. To be intellectual is to think conceptually, which is to say that specifically intellectual activity means the practise of applying general truths to particular situations. No persons whatever are more persistently and habitually intellectual than the uneducated and unintelligent average man. The application of proverbs and the proverbial attitude of mind generally is, for instance, thoroughly intellectualist. "You can't touch pitch without being defiled"; "Tell me who your friends are and I'll tell you what you are"; "Take care of the pennies and the pounds will take care of themselves"; these and such like ideas do the same kind of mischief in common life, as insufficient abstract propositions do in science and philosophy. Many a man after painfully accumulating his pennies has foolishly lost his pounds; many a man and more women have been ruined for life because they have once touched pitch, even though the pitch has not adhered; many a man has been misjudged because of his companions. A generalisation has been applied to a situation without taking into account the particular circumstances of that situation. It makes no difference whether that generalisation is expressed in terms of the most abstruse abstractness, or in terms most familiar and easy of apprehension. To be intellectual, whether one knows it or not, is to apply general ideas to particular situations. To be intelligently intellectual is to be concerned that the situation is suitable to the integral application of the general idea. For instance, take the proverb that you can't touch pitch without being defiled. Place beside it the other proverb which says that to the pure all things are pure. Intelligently to apply these to a particular case would mean that one notes whether the person in question gives evidence of being defiled, whether the person remains pure, or whether the state is one that lies between these two extremes.

The kind of error that is universal in everyday experience is just as common in what we call the intellectual world, and the care necessary to avoid trouble in the everyday instance must be applied as well to the general ideas which are more clearly recognised as such than are those of the man in the street. Intellectuality is misused when it is not recognised that in a given situation a number of those ideas which modify each other, should be kept in mind. One fails in intelligence when, instead of reckoning with this complexity, one attempts an arbitrary and crude simplification which ignores much of what ought to be considered. Intellectualism is none the less crude because the terms are abstract, and remote from the usages of Tom, Dick and Harry. It is, for instance, crudely intellectual to distinguish things as intellectual merely because the words sound that way, rather than to recognise that this state of mind can just as well be expressed in the most familiar and intimate terms.

Almost everyone will admit that it is well to be intelligent in some circumstances, that it is at times advisable to consider all the relevant facts, and that the conditions of the moment will tell what are the relevant facts to be considered. The facts relevant to consider when you are lost on the mountains in a freezing night, are not the same as those that are relevant to your decision to go up on the mountains. If you are lost and must go on for your life's sake, you are all the better for not thinking of your weak heart, though this should be a relevant fact when you are planning where to walk. One discusses nothing else but ways and means while engaged in a course of action, but before going in one can, if so disposed, consider whether one wants to go into that particular thing at all.

Mankind has made much greater progress in its arrangements for carrying on than it has in its studies of the ends that are desirable. Inevitably it accepts the urge of living things to do something. What is alive is in some sense dressed up for going out, and it has to go somewhere. This is true of man, as it is also true of the amoeba. And since man is intelligent as well as alive, since he looks before and after, since he needs names for things, it comes to pass that he must name, among other things, the places he would go to, the desired ends, the goals. Further, having in general a high conceit of himself, he gives to the remoter, ostensibly the more important of these goals, the prettiest names he can think of—he calls them Ideals.

These ideals easily become objects of worship. They are to most persons not matters to be discussed, but predetermined facts. The conservative, especially, considers himself engaged in a prearranged course of action, for which only details of ways and means can be discussed. He looks on anyone who thinks that the direction can be changed, as impractical, absurd, as lacking in understanding of what is vital and serious in life. The whole of life, his own and society's, is in course, and to question its goal is to question its entire validity. He is not only resolute to keep the goal unchanged, but also, he is very tender of its reputation. He thinks of it as something easily broken and tarnished. It is, by a curious contradiction, for him the most indestructible and the most fragile of things. Like all other gods, it is there for adoration and not for criticism.

In spite of the attempts of conservatives to keep us pointed right, we have gotten so far today that ideals, religious, political, social, are with difficulty kept from the impious hands of those who cannot take a perfectly proper view of things, but the larger aspects and the significance of art remain almost unquestioned. Art is socially important—congressmen, captains of industry, and proletarian revolutionaries, here agree with the aesthetes—and the universal admission seems to make it almost unnecessary for anyone to argue in its favour. Some fear for it, but no one attacks it. Pleas for it are, of course, often made, but these are rarely more than twaddle in substance, rhetorical exhortations in which everything that ought to be proved is assumed. Not only is the importance of art assumed, but it is assumed that everyone knows how and why it is important. Look about you at the growing grass, the gay and gorgeous flowers, the birds that fly and sing; recall the work of the Masters—what would life be without Michelangelo and Titian and Rembrandt, without the Glory that was Greece; and Shakespeare, the Myriad-minded—language here grows limp. Ain't Nature wonderful, and art even more so because it isn't nature, and so on.

When one enquires a little more curiously into all this, the clarity becomes somewhat clouded. One finds that in fact almost everyone likes pretty things and really enjoys them. One finds that very few people, comparatively, like serious art, though a great deal of trouble is taken to make them do so. The same woman who will spend hours in the Magasins de Louvre picking out pretty things to wear, will be herded through the Musée de Louvre as fast as the guide can drive her. She goes there because she has no doubts of the importance of art. Hers not to question why, so she just goes and does it.

The things that people do and how they do them, are more demonstrative of what they genuinely believe and think, than are the things that they say. It is, therefore, more useful to know what are the actual attitudes of people toward art than what are their phrases. Unfortunately, it is also much harder to find out. But as it is not my purpose in this book to carry out an enquiry of this sort, but to deal with the subject that is there involved in a different way, I shall leave this matter with a mere mention, and pass on to things that are easier.

It may be admitted, I think, almost without dispute, that there are three unquestionable goods—health; intelligence, defined as the ability to find your way through or round those situations for which you can get the relevant knowledge; money, or its equivalent, enough of this to keep you from squalor and wretchedness. That health, intelligence, and so much of a competence, are the normal conditions for human activity, and for satisfying human companionship, and that they are simply and directly good, can hardly be disputed. Almost everything else is questionable. Many other things—science, art, industry, administration, the world's work and the world's play, are good, no doubt, but the goods are not simply, directly to be understood as taken. These things are terribly complicated, and the ideas that prevail about them, are mostly of the intellectual kind that I mentioned in the first part of my chapter. They are general ideas which, except for science, are applied without any sufficient attempt to understand their relevance to the actual facts. Something has, to be sure, been done in recent years to make thinking more realistic in respect of most of these matters, but none the less the ideas in use are in large part nothing more than habits generalised to form ideas. Of course their real warrant is no greater than the value of the habit from which they derive. And in many cases where there has been some real thinking that is available for intellectual Sundays and holidays, the workaday, everyday thinking, remains of the habit kind.

Mankind, when these habits began to take form, was like the Montessori children who could very well be left to their own devices. Give them a certain equipment, and they can occupy themselves satisfactorily because their range of possible choice is small. As the children grow older, however, and the range of possible choices becomes greater, there is increasing danger of dissipated energy, of incapacity for choice, and progress. So in man. But he, being driven by the spur of necessity, had to find rules and standards somewhere, and he found them by taking the ideas which his earlier experience had provided him, to be sufficient ideals for ever after. The growing complexity of his knowledge led to a rift between his ideals and his knowing, and this rift has now grown beyond all sufferance.

The twentieth century cannot stand for this kind of thing. Therefore fundamentalism is its great enemy. For fundamentalism is not confined to religion but is found in all lines of interest. Fundamentalism simply means that the house of knowledge can be built on the foundations of ignorance. The general ideas that grew to expression when knowledge was limited, must not be changed. The new wine must be poured into the old wine-skins. You may, if you choose, be intellectual, but you must not be intelligent.

This book is an attempt to be intelligent about aesthetics. It is not concerned to prove anything, but simply to enquire into a state of things. I do not find in the books on this subject that I have read, that the things they treat of hang together in an intelligible way. The authors start with too many assumptions about art, and are unwilling to risk failure. I cannot say of aesthetic values as Stephen A. Douglas said of slavery, that I do not care whether they are voted up or down. My own vote is in their favour. But the slavery question was not satisfactorily settled when slavery was destroyed. The question of aesthetic value is not decided by voting art a good thing. Somehow good and sometimes, no doubt, but how and when.

This book does not purport to be a contribution to science in any exact sense. There is as yet no body of knowledge in matters aesthetic, that is either extensive or precise. We do, indeed, often hear of psychological aesthetics, and experimental aesthetics, and various other brands. But in these the psychology is more in the label than in the facts, and the experiments, though often interesting, are rarely important. I propose to do no more than talk about aesthetics in a very unsystematic way, and with no pretence to be anything more than useful.

The subject matter of aesthetics is, in my opinion, of enormous practical importance, or at least it would be so in a world where intelligence was more generally efficient than it is in the world which we know. Aesthetics, therefore, as the exposition of this subject matter, is also of great possible importance. But it must be made intelligible if there is to be effective propagation. One cannot make it intelligible if one is going to start up psychological rabbits as one's ostensible game, which soon turn to ghosts of rabbits, and a moment after disappear entirely, leaving one to make up the rest of the adventure as best one can. I am going to avoid, as far as possible, this kind of catastrophe. There are lots of classifications in the body of my book. But none of them pretend to be more than useful. I believe that they help to make the subject clearer, but they claim no abstract, no metaphysical, validity.

No one can get much good out of my book who reads it intellectualistically, who undertakes to discuss the classifications dialectically, who, in short, treats the text as though it could stand by itself. My own assumption is that the reader and I are looking at certain things, objects in the outer world, feelings, ideas—all sorts of things—and that I am commenting on them for the purpose of getting him to see them in a way which seems to me desirable, profitable. The commentary cannot stand by itself because a comment assumes acquaintance with its subject matter. It is not enough to have had this acquaintance, to remember the stuff vaguely. The stuff must be actually present. One can, perhaps, get along without the comment, one cannot get along without the things to which the comment refers.

II. On Criticism

T HE HABIT OF A critical interest in art is general among cultivated people, and it is commonly regarded as a superior kind of interest. This seems to me a mistake. Critical interest is, of course, appropriate to certain moments in one's life, but they are moments when one either is preparing to take in a work of art, or when after one has done so, one wants to talk about it. Critical interest leads to a concern for what is good and bad in a work of art, or for what makes up a work of art, and it tends to make it seem that we should reckon with these matters as present factors in getting from the work of art what of best it has to give us. I believe, on the other hand, that the mere ability to tell good art from bad is of the least possible importance so far as anything intrinsically valuable in art is concerned. The ability to make such distinctions has value, so far as I can see, for the market and for conversation. If you buy "good" pictures you are more likely to make money out of them, and for purposes of conversation comparisons are invaluable. "I like the Walrus best," said Alice: "because you see he was a *little* sorry for the poor oysters."

When I said that "the ability to tell good art from bad is not of the least possible importance so far as anything intrinsically valuable in art is concerned," I assumed that art had an intrinsic value, and the reader might ask me here and now to tell what this intrinsic value is. Of course I cannot tell him now, because my whole book is the answer. At present I am standing on the obvious fact that a work of art is something that we use, and that we use things because they have some desirable properties. What this desirable property is cannot be told offhand. It might even be questioned whether we have the knowledge necessary to tell at all. In any case I think that the answer is far from easy, and I am going to discuss this and many other things in my book as though the answer were anything other than certain. Where conventional habits are strong and good reasons surprisingly hard to find, this is the only wise method.

By way of opening, I shall ask what criticism actually is. Obviously criticism is not a simple unitary thing unless we proceed to deal with one kind of thing, calling that criticism, despite the fact that it is not a very sharply distinguished thing. A proper classification requires that the constituted class shall include all of one kind of object, and exclude all objects that are not of that kind. The sharpness of the classification will depend, in part, on the distinctness of the objects. The sharpness in chemistry is, for instance, very great. There is a marked interval between one atomic weight and another. Though it is true that scientists are coming to the conclusion that even here the distinctions are not so absolute as they used to be thought, that measurements of things that are so apparently definite as atoms represent statistical averages and are not measurements of things absolutely alike, none the less the distinctions can be taken as sharply and clearly defined. In our field of criticism no such distinctions are possible. It is doubtful whether anything can be said of criticism in general except that it is made up of statements which affirm, explain, or justify, discriminations. Beyond that any assertions that one can make will contradict something that is valid for some kind of criticism. All that I can do here is to comment on some of the kinds that are usual in matters aesthetic, and to point to their place in our social economy.

Criticism can serve to guide to further production. By getting to know in what respect work already done succeeds or fails, one can direct one's own further work. This is a kind of criticism that artists commonly apply to the things that they see, even when they do not consciously do it for profit. It is not the only kind that they practise, because they are human beings as well as artists, but they do find such criticism important. In former days it was common for critical writers in general to think that their appreciations of art would be of use in directing the artist to the right paths, but this notion is now rather outworn. Critics have come to learn, as the earlier literary art critics had not, that all art production is an intensely technical matter, and that the connection of such general ideas as philosophers possess, with actual works of art, is not as close as philosophers once thought it to be. Therefore the intelligent critic today avoids giving the productive artist good advice. So far as the general public is in view, this kind of criticism is best left out. The lay reader can get from it only that inadequate amount of technical knowledge which leads him to misunderstand a great deal, and which does not further his real understanding at all. Worse than that, it supplies him with more technical jargon than ever the artist uses, and makes his language an offence.

Another kind of criticism is that which judges works of art as good or bad. In its crudest form it tells what are the best books of the year, of the month, of the week; which are the best plays of the season; above all it delights in saying that this thing is better or worse than another. Art critics tell you that so and so's pictures are the best in the show, but not as good as something he did last year or the year before, as though comparing pictures seen at several years' intervals were to them child's play—which in another sense it is.

This kind of criticism at its best attempts to make out why the works of art that the writer prefers are better than others that he does not like so well. In this case a man does not only judge, but tries to prove that his judgment is good and such as all men should agree with. This kind of criticism implies a belief in a special competence that is peculiar to the critic, an ability to judge more rightly than most. When this critic thinks differently from the general mass of people—and if he didn't he would be a discouraged critic—he feels his peculiar rightness as his most valuable asset.

The other critical function which I shall refer to is one that is indistinguishable from what is ordinarily called gossip. Gossip tells what has happened to people; it attempts to analyse their actions; it judges the propriety of what they do; in short, gossip is the result of our interest in people, and of our desire to tell others what we know about them, and to hear what the others know. The only essential difference between this gossip and science is that in science we are careful to state our facts correctly, and to verify our conclusions. When we make statements about doubtful facts, and ignore verification, we know that what we are doing is not significantly scientific.

In the field of criticism this is always the state of the case. Every work of art, no matter what the kind, is a complex unanalysable object, which we have to judge as a whole. Our impressions of it are often very vivid, but they are also variable. What we say about it is never very accurate, and we cannot explain to anyone else very precisely what our impressions are. We do exactly what people do when they gossip about their neighbours. Crude and clumsy people can only narrate incidents and make crass comments upon them, just as they can do no more when speaking of a work of art than to tell what it represents, and whether they like it or not. More subtle gossips can minimise the mere narrative, and elaborately discuss the play of characters, of motives, of consequences. Of course it is all very uncertain. It may come to pass that the most admirable construction of intuition and inference is proved quite false because the persons under review in the case are not of the kind supposed, or else the situation which is postulated is not at all the actual situation.

A precisely analogous thing takes place in criticism. The newer psychology with which everyone today is getting to have some acquaintance, makes it clear how little certain knowledge we have of people, of what they think, and of what they intimately do, and makes it equally clear that the opinions we have of them are an indefensible mixture of simplicity and shrewdness. Our understanding of works of art is not any more certain; it is also sketchy and unreliable, and personal to the last degree. The generalisations about classic and romantic, about national character and the influence of race, about the motives and biases of artists, about the elements in a work of art productive of certain effects, all these things and many others, though solemnly written down by professors and wise men of presumptive dignity, are none the less just the same kind of thing as the gossip that flows forth in an endless stream when anything happens which can win the public ear.

Gossip is an excellent thing, which makes socially interesting many persons and their acts, which would otherwise be undesirable. None the less it is not "the greatest thing in the world," nor is it "what men live by." People are needed as something to talk about, but they are yet more needed for love and friendship, they are more needed to work with and to play with. No one seems to us, in general, more undesired than the inveterate gossip, who has exhausted his co-operation when he has fully expressed his opinion. Co-operative range is, we believe, rather larger than that.

What is true of gossip is also true of criticism. It is entertaining, as gossip is. It is like gossip a means, though a precarious one, toward clarifying and understanding. But a critical attitude toward art is not a goal. To be content with a critical understanding of art is very much like being content with a critical understanding of our food. No one can satisfy his hunger by criticising a menu, or by critically tasting the preparations put before him. Yet this is what people do with art in the proportion that they take it seriously. They criticise it especially when they regard it as important. They attach enormous importance to having the right opinion about it, and they do not often get beyond this.

If one were to speak to them of feeding on it, of assimilating it, they would hardly know what one was talking about.

My purpose in writing this book is precisely to insist upon the importance of the aesthetic experience as something as essentially practical as food. I believe that this matter is not at all bound up with an interest in art as good or bad. Nor have I ever heard a very good reason given why anyone should prefer good art to bad. Since, however, it is commonly taken for granted that people ought to do so, I shall, before I start on my own course, see what others have to say about this.

III. Why Good Art Rather Than Bad

In this chapter i shall examine some of the notions about art that are well thought of today, and ask whether any of them show grounds why good art is more to be desired than bad. If, as I think, it appears that none of them do show any such grounds, I shall be right to set aside this belief as questionable, and can then go forward to study our subject impartially. What I am concerned to find out is the nature of aesthetic experience and its effective value. I am not interested to justify or to combat the prejudices and superstitions that are current with regard to it.

The psychopathologists have worked out and made popular a view of the active character of art in individual and social life which looks on it as essentially a kind of compensation. Life according to them is what Longfellow said it was—it is real and it is earnest, and on the whole very far from pleasant. To compensate for this unpleasantness we imagine a world that is better than ours really is, and so we escape into the other-world of dream, of art, of the neurotic fantasy. According to Rank, "The highest form of the artist—the dramatist, the philosopher, and the religious founder—stands close to the psychoneurotic; the lower forms approach the dreamer."

The artist is superior to the psychoneurotic because his productive process is partially effective. He really does make something that objectively exists. Of course in this respect the artist does not essentially differ from the businessman, the inventor, the traveller, or any other kind of person who gets rid of his inner conflicts by doing something. The principal difference is that in getting rid for the time being of his troubles, he makes something that, in turn, will work in similar fashion upon others. A man who, driven into business to escape his inner troubles, builds a suspender factory, can supply suspenders to the public, but if instead his talents permit him to exercise a literary imagination, he can visit the wide spaces, where his public can follow him and share in his escape, on almost his own terms.

Before the psychopathologists had come to stress the value of art as an escape, the most popular view among the loftier thinkers had been that art—the beautiful—the aesthetic—was man's nearest approach to the absolute. Science was an abstraction, but art was, at the least, an adumbration of the real. The real, whether it was conceived as a system of absolute ideas, or as a restless, ever-hungering will, was most completely apprehended by contemplative passion, a mystic absorption whose character was aesthetic. Only so could man, cabined, cribbed, confined, break from the tentacular clutch of circumstance and touch what things are free from the taint of time, space, and mortality.

Reality which in its fulness escapes the hungering grasp of all except the transcending mystic in the moment when he dies to live, can symbolically, and so mediately, be given to all men, when in beauty they get an echo faint but authentic, the perfume, and the savour, of eternity.

There is something common to these conceptions of the pathologists of the soul and the mystics. The resemblance and the difference call to mind what a well-known cubist painter said after he and I had talked of cubism throughout the length of one long evening. He said that he was much surprised to find ourselves entirely in agreement. He would never have expected it. The only difference, he said, between us was that I believed "that it could not be done," while he believed "that it could be done." So the difference between the psychoanalyst and the mystic is that the former believes the felt reality to be a compensatory illusion, while the mystic believes that the felt reality is real.

The difference can be narrowed somewhat further. Even the mystic would agree that in many cases the felt reality is not real, but he is sure that sometimes it is. He can offer no clear signs by which anyone except an adept can make the distinction. He or someone whose authority he accepts is, of course, able to tell the real from the illusory.

The psychopathologist is in better case. Everybody will admit that he is partly right. He therefore has a bit of solid ground to stand on. It is certain that he is partly right, and he may be wholly right. The mystic, on the contrary, is partly wrong, and he may be wholly wrong. His contention for his partial rightness can be made good only if his testimony is taken on its face value. We can therefore read him out of court, not because his case is bad, but because he cannot prove it. One can believe in him if one is so directed by nature or by teaching, but there is no coercion. He has a large following, but his denial by the sceptic is complete.

The partial rightness of the pathologist makes us turn again to his thesis. We find him claiming that art in all its forms has the essential character of serving as relief, as a fictitious corrective for a world that loves not man, but chasteneth him beyond his power to endure. Man labours to transform this world, but the real results are less than his demand. The balance he makes up in fiction.

If the claim is true that art is *essentially* fictitious, then its real value stands or falls with the value of fiction. One cannot apply to it tests applicable only to the real. If the value of art is to make us feel good when otherwise we should feel badly, what standards can there be of good art and bad art, and what difference can it possibly make whether the art we choose is good, bad, or indifferent? The question is enormously important. Teachers and critics deride the bad and acclaim the good or what they think is such; an enormous fuss is made all the world over about good art and bad. (I accept for present use the common standards. Good is the accepted good, accepted by the competent, and bad is the rejected. Where there is no jury-unity, the interim verdict stands: not proven.) If art is compensation, why should people like what is good and avoid what is bad? If I am to have compensation, the important thing, it would seem, is that the compensation should compensate. But what compensation does the average man find in the art which makes happy the elect, an art which bores him or, at the best, is just intelligible enough to make him understand why others like it? His only compensation then is to feel himself one of the elect, and this is only indirectly compensation through art.

If we hold with the mystic that the felt value is not delusive, nothing is changed so far as good or bad art is concerned. If beauty brings us in some sense in contact with reality, then the important thing should be the contact. Good mystics often like bad art, and who is of authority to deny them? The mystic test of beauty must be practical.

Beauty is what beauty does, and unless one bring into the argument some other reasons, there the matter rests.

The question, Why good art? is puzzling as it is important. I have been trying for twenty-five years to find a reason for the affirmative answer and have not found one yet within the bounds of the usual discussions. However, we shall look a little longer at the reasons that are given, to learn what others say.

Some will hold that good art is uplifting, broadening, an enrichment of the spirit, and they will tell what happens when one reads Dante or Goethe or Aeschylus, when one looks at the ceiling of Michelangelo, or listens to Beethoven's symphonies. Even if we supposed that appreciation of these things had such an effect, which it perhaps sometimes has but not often, that would not get us very far. Boccaccio is good art as well as Dante, Fragonard as well as Michelangelo, Chopin as well as Beethoven, though none of these would satisfy stern moralists. There is no common line of cleavage, for good and bad art, and for the art which is socially desirable and undesirable.

There are those who stress the value of art as liberating, and point to the effect on Carlyle of Goethe, on John Stuart Mill of Wordsworth, on modern men of Ibsen and Shaw. This effect is real, but it is not an effect of art but the effect produced by certain men who happened to be artists. Kant and Emerson did a like thing with philosophy, and Darwin with science. If something is an effect of art, then the effect will be produced for just the reason that art is art. People constantly forget that illustration and proof are very different things. Whenever a man attains to an unusual age, many persons hurry to him to ask what he did to live so long. He tells them, and they are impressed, but they do not stop to think of all the persons who did the same thing and died young. The absurdity of drawing conclusions of this kind in such instances, is obvious to every intelligent person, but in ethics, aesthetics and the like, no other method is in common use. But it will not do. One must not play fast and loose with one's assertions. If one makes a statement about the effect of art, it must apply to all art. If this is not what one means, then one ought to say what one means, and not use phrases which when enquired into are found to be without any particular meaning.

If art is not necessarily, as art, a moral force, is it a civilising force? That interpretative, formative, expressive energies of men have used art forms as a medium, that possibly sheer energy takes such a form, we may admit, and there was a prescientific era where this sort of expression had a great importance. Of course, the conventional defences of poetry absurdly exaggerate this. They would have us believe that because verse was a characteristic mnemonic form, because work was done to rhythmic chants and so on, therefore art was more characteristically than science the primitive mental habit. But this is certainly false. Science was the primary interest, the attempt through analysis to control nature. Fortunately for their art expression, the analysis of the primitive mind did not go very far. A witch was a more important unit than a chemical atom. Control was exercised through ceremonial, and not by adding reagents to a mixture. It sounds like poetry but was really statement of supposed fact. It is picturesque science and bad science, but it is science.

Art is intrinsically more a socially conservative than a socially disruptive action. We think of it as socially disruptive because it popularises science. Left to itself it habitually recurs to lost simplicities, to primitive states of feeling which are being overlaid by the complications of invention. Art invents more by going backwards than by going forwards. Art as a civilising force works more by influencing those that lag behind than those that push ahead. In our civilisation art belongs especially to the young and the old, to those who have not yet begun to act, and to those who are past action.

There is no ground whatever for supposing that good art is more a civilising force than bad art. The Bushmen do some wonderful drawing. The sculpture of West African negroes gave the strongest aesthetic thrill of recent years. But I have never heard the suggestion made that the importance for the civilisation of the native tribes is more or less great depending on the artistic worth of the cultural objects.

A view that finds favour in some places today, asserts that art to be the best which most adequately expresses most of human values. I think that this is true. I also think it true that the bigger jar will hold the greater quantity of water. It will, in fact, hold the greater quantity of anything you wish to put into it. But usually when we are forced to choose we cannot choose between the more or less of one kind of thing, but between different kinds of things. Rembrandt gives more than Bol or Backer for he gives nearly all that they do, and more. But Rembrandt does not give what Watteau does, nor Renoir. There are directions of personal want that come into the open with a demand for that which Watteau gives which are not satisfied by Rembrandt. Besides that, there was a time when Rembrandt was held in lower estimation than men who today are thought to be greatly his inferiors. These changes in taste are decisive as against the critics. Critics are amazingly simple-minded, and cannot believe that any scale of values is so true as theirs. Yet all the evidence is against them. Raphael was for three centuries the Prince of Painters. Then he became, for many, the Prince of Potboilers. I think it is quite true that the best art expresses most adequately the most of human values, but until that very clever person comes along who can tell us not only of the human values but can judge of their most adequate expression, this statement will remain what it is now—an empty truism.

The educational value of art with special reference to painting has recently been acclaimed in somewhat novel terms. The general idea is, of course, old. The special terms are new. "For to make of paintings an educational means is to assert that the genuine intelligent realisation of pictures is not only an integration of the specialised factors found in the paintings as such, but is such a deep and abiding experience of the nature of fully harmonised experience as sets a standard or forms a habit for all other experiences. In other words, paintings when taken out of their specialised niche are the basis of an educational experience which counteracts the disrupting tendencies of the hard-and-fast specialisations, compartmental divisions and rigid segregations which so confuse and nullify our present life."*

This is a quite amazing bit of ideology. Everybody knows that in a simple system of mechanical forces a new stimulus brings about adjustments that are calculable. The system can reorganise in a few ways only, and consequently the additions of new elements will not be likely to leave the system without obvious change. But when the system is internally complex, it is extraordinarily effective as a shock-absorber. It may undergo internal adjustments of such a kind that the stimulus which had been applied with intent utterly to alter its outward behaviour, produces no change commensurate with the stimulus.

Man's systems of organic mental response are the most complicated that we know, and as shock-absorbers they are effective beyond all whooping. Mankind has managed to preserve the larger part of his primitive mentality despite all that has persuasively and *convincingly* been offered to him for thousands of years. When someone says that "the genuine intelligent realisation of pictures will set a standard or form a habit for all other experience" it is hard to believe that he is serious. A little microbe in a man's intestine may cause the man's death, because it grows and multiplies. It will take a lot of growing and multiplying for an "intelligent realisation of pictures to set a standard" for anything whatever, and one would like to see a demonstration or two

---

* John Dewey, in the *Journal of the Barnes Foundation*, April, 1920.

of the reality of this process, before one gives much credit to the doctrine.

One more account of art and we have done with this subject. There is the view that art is the response to a specific emotion. This specific emotion is apparently strong in some persons, and weak or actually deficient in others. Nature, it would seem, was so solicitous that art should not go unappreciated, that it invented a special emotion which it entrusted to a chosen few. These persons can react more or less ecstatically to the specific stimulus of significant form. They know good art from bad because they are the carriers of the emotion. Its possession implies nothing further about them. They may be virtuous or wicked, intelligent or stupid. The possession of the capacity for this specific emotional response is otherwise as impersonal a matter, as though they were the carriers of typhoid germs.

This view is probably nonsense, since there is not the slightest reason for believing in this peculiar emotion. But the doctrine has the merit that while it does not explain anything, it does not pretend to explain much. It says that certain persons know good art when they see it, and also that they know that they are the persons that know. It's as easy as that.

Except for its explanations this view is, I think, closer to the facts than any other. There is no evidence that the appreciation of good art has any further consequences that hang together in a single system, and which can be distinguished from the consequences of other acts. If the theory of an aesthetic emotion were tenable, this doctrine would make aesthetics the easiest subject for solution among the sciences of man, the paradise of the amateur. Unfortunately it is not tenable. It suggests, however, that we had better look into this question of emotion.

IV. Emotion and Feeling

IT IS THE COMMON belief that art has some very special connection with pleasure, but this is doubtful. The amount of pleasure that people get from art is greatly exaggerated, for though sometimes it gives great pleasure yet it is possible thoroughly to appreciate a great work of art without so much of positive pleasure as one gets from a good stretch. People very commonly realise, to the extent of their capacity, the quality in things, find them good, interesting, valuable or whatever, without finding them very amusing. One could empty almost any art gallery with a nice thrilling accident enacted before its doors. Gambling, horse-racing, baseball, gossip, eating and drinking, and many other things, usually give more pleasure than any kind of art other than that in which these things enter as ingredients. Of course, the art that is crudely compensatory, gives great pleasure to the shop-girl hungry for love and luxury, to the clerk hungry for adventure, to the repressed man hungry for rich human relations. It is hard to drag a child from its stories, or to distract a man from a thrilling novel, but if you interrupt him while he is reading a book of poems or start to gossip in a picture gallery, you are not often repulsed. There are not many whose attention does not wander when they listen to music, or who can look at architecture closely without an effort. If pleasure-giving is the distinctive virtue of art, then art, except for the crudely compensatory, the self-decorative and luxurious, the music that thrills to a kind of action, and the comic and the plaintive, ranks quite low among human interests.

Books on aesthetics do not usually say much about this sort of thing, but their writers are in most cases rather careless about facts. They are almost always out to make a case for art. They accept the masterpieces and their imputed importance. They pay attention to some characteristics of the art experience or the art object, without much concern for similar characteristics in related experiences and objects, outside the field of art. Of course they often do refer to these in a general way, but do not follow out the consequences very far, or very thoroughly. As a result they attribute many qualities to art as such which are not peculiar to it. They make definitions which are not true—this is pardonable— and which are also useless. I never read a book on aesthetics without a feeling of irritated restlessness at the way in which the obvious facts are ignored, at the way in which solutions that obviously do not solve are accepted as though they did, at the way in which the author is bound to go through whether there is any thoroughfare or not. I fear for my book that it will be heavy and dull because I do not want to do this. If I cannot reach a genuine goal, I would rather remain forever on the way.

I believe that the first cause why there is so much confusion in the treatment of these subjects is that emotion is thought to have some special connection with aesthetics. It is obvious, of course, that emotions are more attended to when we have no other response to an exciting cause than just to see it, but this does not mean that emotions specially belong to that situation. One who looks at a picture will often have stronger emotions than the man who painted it; the spectators at a game will be more emotionally stirred than the players; the audience at the theatre than the actors. This is not always the case, but it is commonly so. Most painters when they try to make a picture are perfectly cool. They try to see, and it is not excitement they are looking for. This is not always true. Sometimes because a vivid impression is gotten suddenly, or because there is a struggle to get it at all, the emotional reaction is intense. Sometimes when the impression is tangled in repressed material there is a strong emotional accompaniment. But this emotional excitement is not essential either to art production or its appreciation. If it were, it would always happen, and it cannot be too often repeated that what belongs to art always happens where art occurs. What only happens sometimes is not essential, and is almost always something that happens also when there is no art. There is nothing in any way peculiar to the relation of emotion to art, though there are cases when that which is peculiar to art and that which is peculiar to emotion come together. For example, a person with a strongly felt emotion may write a poem or heave a brick. Another time he may do the one thing or the other, because the situation makes upon him that demand. Neither the heaving of bricks nor the writing of poems is an essentially emotional act. They are modes of response with no such fixed conditions for their occurrence.

The root falsity found in all views of the kind here rejected is, I think, the assumption that emotions can be classified, that they can be discriminated because of special characters in different emotions. Some believe that there are quite a lot of different emotions. Some believe that there are only three. I doubt very much that there is more than one, which is just emotion. I have been studying emotional reactions very closely for a number of years in what are practically experimental conditions, and I can find no certain evidence that there are even two. What seems like multiplicity of emotions, is the colouring of the emotion by factors that blend with the emotion, but are not of it.

I have found in studying conflicts, repressions and so on, that it is quite possible to have an intense emotional disturbance which has no definable character other than that of being emotion, on condition that the skeletal muscles remained at rest, or continued undisturbed their indifferent movements, such as walking. I have often started something going in my mind, a process intended to make it easier to admit to observation something that I preferred not to observe. Very often the effort would not succeed, and for a time my mind would remain almost blank except for the consciousness of the effort, and the shifting recurrence of the ideas which would not remain in the focal centre. I often found it well, after continuing this for a while, to half turn my attention elsewhere, possibly to a book, which I read with the corner of my eye on the conflicting situation. It would happen again and again that after some minutes, an emotional stress would begin, and persist sometimes for very long periods. There have been cases where the emotional response did not come on for ten minutes or more after direct attention had been withdrawn from the conflict.

It was invariably the case that this emotion had no particular character. Whether the theme was definitely erotic, whether it had to do with fear, or anger, made no difference to the quality of the emotion. On the other hand, an adjustment of the skeletal muscles, even those of the larynx and throat, in the appropriate attitudes, would at once give to the emotion a similar colouring. It is obvious enough why it should be generally thought that the emotions have in their essence this diversity. Usually a situation leads to a responsive attitude in which the emotion arises. When I first began to do this sort of thing, my emotions were of different kinds, because I responded to the thought with more definite muscular reactions. It was only when I maintained the bodily poise practically unaltered, that I began to obtain these indeterminate emotions.

It is common to find careless statements about the emotions in the writings of psychologists, even in the writings of those who are very "scientific." J. B. Watson in *Behaviorism*, says that "Cannon has brought out the facts that in fear and rage behaviour, digestion and absorption are often completely interfered with—food is left in the stomach to ferment. ... Love behaviour, on the other hand, seems usually to heighten metabolism. Digestion and absorption apparently take place more rapidly ... after normal sex intercourse hunger contractions begin in the stomach and food is very frequently sought."

It is really so evident that it ought not to have been overlooked, that Cannon's animals, confined and irritated to show fear and rage, are very different from persons enjoying natural intercourse, and it is rather a hasty judgment that would impute all the consequences to the difference between rage or fear, and love. A man can rage merrily and sit down hungry to his dinner if he has thoroughly discharged his temper, while instances where appetite is lost and food is indigestible for those in love, are exceedingly common. Sustained excitement often has this effect. A few minutes ago I got indigestion while eating my lunch alone though I was perfectly happy and cheerful, because I chanced to think about something too intensely and at too rapid a tempo. Constraint or freedom in action is probably more important in determining consequences of these kinds, than is the supposed kind of emotion. Conditions of constraint, and many other things, cut in all sorts of ways across the conventional classifications of emotions.

Facts like these reinforced the personal experiences described in the preceding paragraphs, and the two things together led me to discriminate between feelings and emotions. Emotion is just emotion, while feelings are as numerous as appropriate adjustments. They can be grouped, but the groups have no hard and fast limits. They are merely convenient. Of course those who believe in the instincts as rather definite types of reactions, will readily class the emotions according to their colouring by the attitude-feelings of the instincts. For those who think that instincts are of not much use when one is studying man, this way of classifying will, again, be merely a convenience.

That the distinction between feelings and emotions is a valid distinction will, I think, be clear if we consider the difference in reaction time between the striped and unstriped muscles. The unstriped muscles are much slower. When we have a frightening shock we respond at once. We feel frightened, but it is noticeable that the vascular disturbances often come on slowly afterwards. Often the person under strong emotion will say, I was so frightened, that is, the perception having come which set aside the fear, the emotion continues as mere emotion. We continue to speak of it as fear, but in fact it is no such thing.

What then is feeling? Feeling is perception that cannot be rendered focal. Whenever we see a thing distinctly we call the process *seeing*, but when we see it vaguely, we speak of *feeling* it there. We *feel* that there is something ahead of us in the fog, but when the fog lifts we *see* it. It makes no difference what the nature of the object is, whether it is an idea, an external thing, or an internal thing, the distinction between feeling and perception is merely a matter of clearness.

This difference in clearness has important consequences. What is not clear but is closely associated with what is clear, can easily be assimilated to it. It is treated as a property of that thing, since in itself it tends to be lost, although its effect remains. But a clearly perceived object which is assimilated to another clearly perceived object will not be lost in it completely, but will become its symbol. When, to ring the last of these changes, an object which is clearly perceived, is assimilated to that which is felt only, we have the disparition, the diffusion of the concrete object, which is a characteristic of mystical states. All this stuff will be given a more thorough treatment later. Here it is mentioned only for the purpose of showing why we cannot be satisfied with the common notions that are at present current about emotions.

There is another meaning of the word *feeling* that I have not yet considered. *Feeling* is a term which often is confined to pleasure and unpleasure, formerly called pain. These seem to me only special cases of feeling in general. They are the felt conditions of acceptance or rejection. We do not feel that two and two are four and are not five, we see that it is so. But we feel a maladjustment here and there. A man will say, I don't see just what is wrong but I feel that there is something. This sense of the word *feeling* will also require our attention later.

One word more about emotion. Emotion can, beside its quality of heightening our feelings, enter into the composition of feeling as an element. This means that the emotion can be used to carry us beyond itself to further objects into which the emotion enters as an ingredient. Emotion then becomes something that needs to be expressed, and is not merely the consequence of an experience or of expression. There is, in mental life, a great deal of this sort of multiplex relation, which makes impossible any too neat formulation of its action.

The considerations on emotion and feeling that I have summarily presented are not offered as an argument for my views. I intend to use these terms in the given sense, because they are practically convenient for my purposes. But my primary intent in raising this discussion, was to point out that no doctrine of the emotions and the feelings is generally accepted. There is nothing generally accepted in psychology which is of use for aesthetics except its general direction. Psychology is fairly committed to the view that mind is dynamic, that its conditions are those of action and not reception, or rather that even its receptivity is actively selective. Everything else is in dispute. I think it foolish to make a subject like aesthetics dependent on theories which are not sufficiently convincing to convince anyone except their authors. But if a certain way of thinking of the elements that one must use is useful, and makes one's treatment more serviceable for one's ulterior purposes, it is the way of thinking that one should employ. My psychology is not intended to justify my aesthetics, but rather the reverse. If my aesthetics is good for anything, it may help to justify my psychology.

V. Objects and Instruments

Aesthetics is not concerned especially with emotions, but with that which stands in the extreme opposition to them. It is concerned with objects of a kind. Therefore the next few chapters must deal with kinds of objects, with the degrees to which things have objective character, and with the differences in objective characters.

There is one kind of difference in objects which is very apparent and had better come in for mention at once, since it otherwise will cause unnecessary confusion. This is the difference between ideas, and what we commonly call things. Things are what we encounter, ideas are what we project. In a sense we often encounter our ideas and sometimes bump up against them very hard, but none the less we take them to be things that have been projected, either with intention or else we-know-not-how. When there is actual doubt whether an object has been encountered or projected, we have to do with possible hallucination.

I mention this distinction between things and ideas, so that we may at once put it out of our way. For us the distinction is of no importance. An aesthetic object may be either a thing or an idea, and henceforth, in order to avoid unnecessary elaboration in statement, I shall use the word thing whether the object is really a thing in the ordinary sense, or whether it is an idea. Its thingness for my purpose is its capacity to have objective character.

But not all things can be objects to serve the uses of aesthetic experience. Some things are instrumental, and as instrumental, a thing has not the kind of objectivity with which we shall be concerned. Everyone knows that the less we are conscious of our instrumental means, the easier it is for us to get our effects. The objects that we are to be concerned with in aesthetics, are objects of which we are vividly aware, but first we must deal with the other kind of object which we are not specially interested to keep in the very centre of our vision.

The present chapter and the next are to a large extent preliminary to the definition of what is aesthetic. Therefore they have a little the effect of irrelevance. But this is not really the case. One cannot know a thing satisfactorily, merely by knowing what it positively is. The aesthetic object is not one that can be accurately defined in any possible terms of description or measurement. Therefore it is important to make clear its difference from other things. The aesthetic object is peculiar, which means that it has properties that belong to it, and to no other, and these properties are furthest removed from those that are characteristic of the instrumental things. I shall begin with the examination of the things that have the minimum of objective character, and go through to those that have this character at its maximum, for only in this way will it be possible to bring out fully the importance of the aesthetic, an importance that I believe to be both great and thoroughly practical.

For purposes of contrast to things that have a lesser degree or different kind of objective character, I shall forestall the eventual complete definition of the pure aesthetic object by saying that it has three properties—it is *known*; it is *unified*; it *endures*, that is, it is not consumed by use. Whatever has these properties as constitutive, is an aesthetic object. But before we can reach its thorough description we shall have to look at many things which have some of these properties, or have them all partially and subordinately. The aesthetic object is one to which they give its essential character. The instrument is one which lacks them all.

A good example of an instrument is the air we breathe. We breathe it continually, our life depends upon our utilising the oxygen in it, but under ordinary conditions we are entirely unaware of it. It has no unity, but is a fragmented stream. It does not endure, but is consumed in the body and rejected in an altered form.

Cases which are less extreme but where things have a low grade of objectivity occur in all our habitual actions. We take a bit of bread from the table and put it in our mouths, with nothing more as a directive than a vague impression of something there. What determines the action is that we-are-eating. We often look at a watch and note that the hour has come to do something or has not come, yet if we are asked the time we cannot say what it is. In this case the objective character of the watch dial is of the slightest. It serves to determine a subsequent action, but in itself is hardly noted.

The air, the bread, the watch dial, in the illustrations, have all of them the character of instruments. They are nothing more than means to a further step in the process of utilisation. The breath is taken quite unconsciously, the other things less unconsciously, and from these we can go on to other instruments like telescopes or lathes or automobiles, which in far greater measure hold our attention. But essentially there is no difference. We aspire to the stars, and not to the means. We want to reach a destination, to move rapidly, and the car is just a carrier. Of course one may be interested in handling the car rather than in using it for transportation, but in that case its instrumental character has been changed.

An instrument is something that need not be centrally focused, and furthermore it need not endure beyond the moment of service. Civilisation depends so largely upon the existence of semi-permanent instruments that impermanence does not seem an instrumental character. Air and food are, of course, consumed in use, and so, obviously, are all the substances that enter into chemical products. It is not so obvious that other instruments are likewise passing things.

Let us begin with a self-evident example of a transitory instrument, a match. A match is struck once, and is done for. In this it differs from a hammer. But if we consider, it does not so differ essentially. If a hammer went to pieces at every stroke as a cartridge does at every discharge, the driving of nails would be tedious, and their use would not be practicable. But in principle nothing would be changed. Almost all instruments wear out with use. Their consumption is rapid or slow. And even in those cases where as with the lens there is no structural alteration with use, endurance beyond the moment of use does not belong to the nature of the thing as an instrument.

There is another kind of instrument which is not a pure instrument. A nail, for instance, differs from a hammer inasmuch as it becomes a part of the structure whose parts it holds together. It differs from food which is assimilated to the body but which in the process undergoes dissolution and reconstruction. A nail remains a nail even while it is part of a box. Its dual character can be well realised if we think of it in terms of service, or in terms of time. If we think of it as something that holds the boards together, or that will last for so long or not last, we are thinking of it as an instrument, but if we take the box for just a box, then all its parts are also box. In so far forth the nail is not an instrument.

That instruments are not essential unities is evident, for in their character as instruments they are transitional stages in a process. They are essential only as parts of a whole.

The perfect attitude toward the instrument is to notice it as little as possible. We look where we strike and disregard the muscles; we keep the eye on the ball rather than on the club; we attend to the road and not to the car. But when something goes wrong, this focal interest changes. Then the muscles, the club, the car, may demand our most particular attention. It is when an instrument ceases to work as an instrument, or has not yet become one and is only in the process of making, that it gets to be an object.

This familiar fact shows the way for passing from the notion of the instrument to the notion of the object, and it will eventually lead us all the way to the aesthetic object. Even so we shall never leave the instrument entirely. Even the aesthetic object will prove to be an instrument for the ultimate purpose, which is the journey through life with a possible goal and with certain transitional moments. But so far we have had to do only with the instrument which we subordinated to the process within life. The process of life as a whole will need to be taken up later.

When an instrument ceases to be availably an instrument, it checks us in our tendency to go on doing whatever we are doing. If food is not at hand we cannot take and eat it. The baby's milk is ready prepared for him, and when he is hungry he need merely suck. If this went on throughout his life, he would need as little consciousness of milk as an object as he has of the air. Making sucking motions when he is hungry would automatically restore him. The milk would just happen. But as soon as obstacles have arisen to this simple life, he must concern himself with the object on which he would feed. The obstacle to their immediate use makes instruments become objects as well. In order to get hold of something that is not immediately available, we must keep our attention fixed upon it. We have to distinguish it from other things. We have to keep it in mind. It gets to have the quality of standing by itself. It must more or less endure. It must become in a complete sense, an object.

The thing may, however, remain an object only for a short time. Once seized upon it may be consumed, and done for. Its individual persistence, though actual, may not be permanent. We shall have to note many kinds and degrees of persistence, depending on the kind of obstacle to consumption.

I shall lay great stress upon the different obstacles to consumption, and the objects that are made in consequence. Making and manipulating objects is the business of intelligence. This conception will carry us farther than any other that I know.

One kind of instrument should be noted in passing, because it is peculiar in that endurance is of its essence. This kind includes weights and measures. If these did not endure they would be meaningless. If they are instruments in the same sense as the other things that have been mentioned, they would prove the classification that I have made to be glaringly defective. In fact they are instruments of an entirely different kind.

A thing that is weighed or measured is not altered thereby. It is merely named in a certain way. A large room is more specifically entitled when it is said to be twenty feet long and fifteen feet wide. A heavy man in a particular case is a man of two hundred and ten pounds. So it is always when things are subjected to standards of weights and measures. The things remain what they were in themselves, and are not even altered to the senses as when they are seen through optical instruments. Only our knowledge of the things is altered. Therefore weights and measures belong primarily to the cognitive and not to the instrumental class of things. Cognitive facts have an instrumental character also, inasmuch as through extension of knowledge they lead to reactive effects on things. But this is a subject to be dealt with at the end rather than at the beginning of this treatise.

VI. Object Making

OBSTACLES TO IMMEDIATE CONSUMPTION will be presented in five classes.

1. Obstacles that interpose because the thing is hard to get.
2. Obstacles that interpose because there is fear.
3. Obstacles that interpose because there is foresight of future needs.
4. Obstacles interposed by rules of procedure.
5. Obstacles that interpose because we have need of things that are not consumed by use.

These groups are not biologically conceived, nor are they scientifically valid. They do not pretend to stand for evolutionary classes, nor are they mutually exclusive. They are no more than conveniences of exposition and will, I believe, serve to make clear the meaning of aesthetics.

It is obvious that a thing that must be sought, that must be hunted after, that must be gotten despite all difficulties that lie in the way, is a thing to get itself particularly noticed. Especially is this the case when the pursuer is a seeing animal. The nose is the peculiar organ of instinct. It enables the pursuer to follow and to find, but the object remains vague in any other sense than that of being the desired object. One is enabled to attain and seize the thing, rather than to isolate and to distinguish it. An animal that follows a scent does not, probably, pay much attention to what else lies in the field, even in the immediate field, except when this distracts it. Scent is mainly selective. But sight can perceive both the object specifically sought, and the background against which it stands. It is particularly the sense for objectification.

When it happens, therefore, that a creature in which sight is highly developed has occasion to keep continuously in mind something that it seeks, that something will get to have a growingly greater individuality and distinctness. Furthermore the conditions of the pursuit will make for creation of many other objects. Conditions of the road to attainment get to be particularised and classed, and making the tools that further the quest comes to be of focal interest. A world of objects come into existence, because the thing desired is hard to get.

The character of difficulty as a maker of objects extends to objects of all kinds. I make a class of it because there are so many instances where difficulty in getting stands quite by itself, but in all groups that follow, difficulty in getting, whether imposed or sought for, enters as an element.

The second class of objects due to an obstacle is that of objects that are made by fear. Fear, as an obstacle, has played a great part in the history of man. The simplest reaction to a fearful object is, of course, to run away without enquiring further. But often one wants the thing of which one is afraid, and still more often one wants something else despite the fearsome thing. This may lead to the creation of objects similar to those produced by simple difficulty. But there is one class of objects in great part produced by fear that is of special interest. These are objects of fantasy. Unrealisable desires also produce their fantasies, but it is fear in conflict with desire that is the strongest stimulus and the richest source. The importance of this kind of thing for art has been stressed, perhaps overstressed by the psychoanalysts. Here we can spend only a few words upon it.

Desires that fear to culminate in act, are common in men. All men will risk something to gain their ends, but there are almost always limits to the risks that men will take. One who will risk his life will not risk his reputation. Another who can face danger cannot face ridicule. One who will enquire boldly into what lies before him, will shrink from enquiry into what lies behind him. Yet all these persons, and most others, want results that are not possible to get if they surrender to their fears. There are also the great fears common to men in groups, culminating in the master fear of death. For all these fears men seek compensations. They seize on hints to which they give unreal values, and exaggerated importance. They build up structures of fantasy in some of which they truly believe, but in many others they disbelieve without believing in their disbelief. The structures of fantasy get to have a kind of independent existence, for their authors have renounced, or have not recognised, their creations. Yet in these creations much of their life is lived, and through them they grow to be other, and often more, than in themselves they are.

Even before the systematic studies of recent years it was well known that wish fulfilments play a big role in religion and art. What we cannot do or fear to do, god or the devil, the hero or the villain, does for us. That which threatens us, gets its appropriate symbol.—What would prohibition have done without the Demon Rum!—All requirements find their fulfilments, and reach expression in appropriate objects. We expand into a world of our own fabrications, and remake the other world to still our fears. The scapegoat is a sacrifice for our lesser sins, and we seek salvation on the vicarious cross of a crucified God.

The third class of objects is that which grows from voluntarily deferred consumption. The arid future throws its shadow on the abundant present, and leads to preparation for the time of dearth. Saving, as we have all been taught, makes capital, and capital, if not itself creative of civilisation, is the material basis of civilisation.

The future is almost entirely a remembered thing. It is constructed and not found. Probably, the only actually felt future is the ever and ever receding terminus of the living present. But the future is not a simply transposed past, it is remade for the purpose. When someone, thinking of his blundering conduct in some past affair, dramatically makes it over in his mind, he rethinks the past as he now would like to remember it. He relives the past, in so far as he begins it over again at some moment that has now elapsed, and brings it to a conclusion at some time before the present. If, however, he should place the reconstruction in another temporal period; if instead of a fancied remaking of the past he should begin it now or look upon it as a plan to meet a similar occasion in the future; if, to go a step further, he should actually arrange for such a future; then the remembered fact as reworked in the present, becomes, as planned, a memory of a hypothetical future; to be later realised as present; and in conclusion, once more, remembered as a past. All planning, all prophesying, is virtually a transposed, remembered, past.

This is the thing that happens when the remembered fear of dearth leads to a reconstructed future memory of plenty. Imagination is largely a transposed memory-action, whereby we place ourselves at the conclusion of an unexpired moment, and remember that which never was, but might or ought to have been. It is the occasion for infinite invention, for unlike the pressure of an immediate need which does not give us time to look about us and reflect, it has the values of an active leisure. This subject is so interesting that one would like to amplify it further, but as it lies upon our road and is not a part of our goal, I shall have to leave it with these few inadequate sentences.

My fourth class is a most interesting one. It is the class of things that come to being, because a given end may be reached only after certain rules have been complied with. This makes the essence of a game. There are instances where rules are made for convenience only, and are not essential to the situation. One may have a private secretary and need no rules of governance at all. He does his work as he finds it most convenient, and that is all that is required. Rules become necessary when a large office force must get similar results. But for a game a rule is of the essence of the matter. When Huck Finn said, "I don't enjoy my vittles 'thout they're tollable hard to get," he told of making a game of eating. Huck was an active and inveterate loafer, a boy who had no obligations. He was in no danger of starvation. He might have let things happen, and picked the profits. But an active person requires obligations, and if they do not come to him he goes to them. For Huck eating was an ideal occasion. It had the merits of a strong stimulus—hunger, a short term of remission, and an ample satisfaction. The rules were not complicated, in fact there was only one, that the food should be tollable hard to get, but that rule made of eating a game, and added zest to life.

Huck's life was not the ordinary one, for it was all vacation, but for the ordinary man, vacation creates similar conditions. While he is working he likes to have his meals served regularly and without trouble to himself, but when he is camping he does not enjoy his vittles 'thout they're tollable hard to get. Only starvation will make him break the rules against pot-hunt procedure. Eating has for the time being become a game.

In every case a game has this particularity that the ostensible end is not the real one. It is not to get the ball across the plate, nor to touch the ground behind the goal-posts, nor to reach the top of the mountain, nor to take the cards away from your neighbour, that is important, but to do this thing in accordance with certain rules.

The man who cheats does not play the game, but more than that, he does not play at all, because he sets the end to be itself the desired consummation, and so negates the essentials of a game.

Playing and creative activities are essentially opposed. Creation is the making of something, and the thing to be made is the only intrinsic term. The player, as such, cares nothing for the end, except as the last term of a regulated process.

Play is generally looked on as distraction, and that is literally its role. Huck Finn was a boy who needed distraction. He was too active to take life easily, he was necessitated to nothing, and his creative interests were slight. In this respect he differed notably from Tom Sawyer. Therefore he needed the diversion of play. Tom invented games, but Huck for the most part just played them. In fact, he was so realistic-minded that he hardly understood the nature of his principal employment, and in this he did not differ very much from many estimable people.

Play is properly a divergence from the course of serious things, and in a rational world it would be this and nothing more. When a boy is bored in going on an errand and steps carefully on alternate stones in the pavement, or leaves the pavement at the crossings with the right foot and gets on with the left, he knowingly diverges from the business of life, to its distraction. But when etiquette ceases to be a convenience and becomes a solemn drag, it is a game played by players who don't know a game when they see it. Etiquette begins as a rule of order, then becomes a game, and often ends as ritual and religion. When it ceases to be a rule of order, it gets to have the specific value of making ends more remote. A thing not worth having is made to seem valuable by distance. It is a part of the "conspicuous expenditure" of time and money, that compensates a man for being rich.

Objectification comes about from games, because the attention is turned to incidents that make the stages in the progress toward the end. If we play at touching the alternate rails of a fence, the individual rails get to have an actual existence for us, that they lack when we just pass along the street. A multitude of objects have been created by and for games, and few things awaken a more acute attention, or lead to more perceptive discrimination.

Play, like most things in this world, is not free from contamination. Other things are commonly mixed with it. Gambling confuses issues, when more interest is taken in the winnings than in the play. The desire to win may make one indifferent to the actual rules as when one cheats, or to the spirit of the rules as when one wants to win even by a fluke. But this kind of distinction is easy to make, at least in principle.

There are other and more interesting cases, like the etiquette already mentioned, where play is made a part of what is not play. Creation, I have said, and play are radically opposed, yet often rules are made for creative activity and come to be believed in as really belonging to it. Rules for the structure of a drama, rules which tell what a picture should be, rules of conduct when conformity rather than virtue is the test, are instances. Conformity, for instance, when not socially serviceable, is essentially a game. Few things would be more liberalising to the mind than learning what is play, and what is not play.

VII. Objects as Known

WE NOW COME TO my fifth class of objects, that of the things we wish both to consume and to conserve. In general this is not practicable with physical things, but there is one kind which is exceptional, the catalysts. These mysterious substances, of which the platinum sponge with which one can light the gas is an example, are capable of causing chemical changes without, apparently, themselves changing. Physical catalysts are not familiar to most of us, but catalysts for the mind are common.

Pippa Passes is a study in catalysis. The little working girl spends her holiday strolling about the town, wondering about the people in it, envious of their good fortune, singing her songs. These songs remain unalteratedly hers, but beyond her, they strike into the complex circumstances of other lives, and change their courses. Anyone may sometime have such effects on others, and there are people who influence markedly the temper of any gathering which they join. They are the catalytic personalities, those whose influence is almost unescapable.

Are all things in so far as they are known catalysts? Yes. These make up my fifth class. For shortness I shall call them cognitive objects.

Cognitive objects are important in many ways. Things as known are the means for redirecting our lives in all the circumstances where intelligence is at work, yet the thing as known is unaltered. Whether it is a material thing, or whether it is an idea, makes no difference. It may be forgotten immediately afterwards, the knowledge may be outgrown and cease to work in us, but in itself it is inviolable. The use to which it has been put has not altered it.

It is likewise true that nothing depends upon the permanence of the object in itself. One may recall a word spoken long ago, a meteor flash across the sky, which came and went in a moment, and equally well one may recall one glimpse of a mountain or a monument, which had been there for ages, and would endure for ages after.

It may seem unreasonable to some to speak of finding an idea which remains unaltered, because they think of ideas as being made by the mind, and that the mind in knowing its ideas, knows itself. I do not discuss this, because it is, for my purposes, of no importance. In practical fact we do not know an idea until we know it, and we then regard it as something fixed which we can put into a dictionary or an encyclopaedia, or that we can record in a picture or a poem. It is thought very wonderful that one can go to sleep with an unsolved problem in one's mind, and wake the following morning with the answer, but it is just as wonderful that we can ask ourselves a question at one moment, and answer it the next. The elapsed time is a detail. In both cases the inexplicable has happened—something new has come into the world. I do not know what is the next word I shall write until I find the word within me, and put it out in writing. All knowledge is found. The difficulty is to create the conditions that will put it there, so that it may be found.

Our fifth class, then, consists of knowledgeable things, of cognitive objects—of things perceived or remembered, and of ideas.

It is our common way to make a very definite distinction between the things that exist outside us, and which impress themselves upon us, and the things that we find in our minds, and which we project as ideas. But for the present purpose the difference between these kinds of things is of no importance. I have no concern whatever with questions of philosophy in this book, but only with questions of practice, and for our practice, what makes a thing to be a particular kind, is the way that it is used in knowledge. All will admit that there is more obvious likeness between a memory and an idea, than there is between a perception and an idea. But to an extent far greater than we commonly think, people are concerned with memories and not with perceptions. The only memories, if it would be proper to call them such, which are perceptions, are after-images. But these hardly ever interest anyone except psychologists. Ordinarily we mean by memories remembered things, and almost always when we think about things, we think about the memories of them. The moment we have heard things said or seen them happen, the moment that we turn away from any sight, we have memories, and memories only, left to deal with.

Two men will often dispute about a picture which is not present to them. One saw it six months ago, the other, two years ago. Neither can be certain how it would look to him if he saw it now. The very discussion they are having might make it look different to one of them if it were here to be seen. Yet, owing to the fact that each one has a memory object which goes back to a preceding period, and which he takes to be the same as the impression which he would get now, the discussion is all but necessarily futile. The conditions for a readjustment do not exist. But so habitual is it to suppose that one is talking about a thing when one is talking about the memory of a thing, that the actual state of the case is either unknown or ignored.

I can in many cases visualise with considerable distinctness pictures that I have not seen for twenty-five years. Of course I know, because reseeing pictures after intervals has told me so, that if I saw them now they would not look to me at all as I remember them. Something is due, of course, to blurring and the modification of the image through the blending of other impressions, but much of the change is due to a change of standards. Like the impressions of the grown man carried over from his boyhood home, the memory image keeps the value relative to formative conditions and cannot, except in theory, adapt itself to the changed status. If critics would always bear in mind that what they say is relative to the moment when they saw the picture, and not relative to the present moment, they could keep their minds free for something better than the justification of their juvenile incapacities.

In a previous chapter I said that aesthetic objects are known, are unified, and are enduring. All cognitive objects are alike for the first and third of these properties, whose discussion must now be brought to a close. Cognitive objects are known and they endure. Changes may take place in us the knowers, and to some extent must take place as the mere result of knowing, but each item of knowledge might conceivably be recorded by an infallible knower who could subsequently recall each past moment in its own appropriate context. That is what we all do with our past knowledge in so far as we can, and our confidence often outruns discretion. The object of knowledge exists by virtue of just this need of referring, and again referring, to it. It exists in definite shape so that it may be held, when the first moment of encounter with it is past. It may be recalled as an integral thing; it may be classed with others of its kind; it may be used in infinite combinations without, by any intrinsic necessity, losing the quality of its particular self. In this sense it is like the cake that is both eaten and kept—it is consumed without forfeit of its immortality. In its essence it is both fleeting and eternal, as swift to pass as the passing thought, as lasting to endure as the travail of creation.

VIII. Scientific and Aesthetic Objects

A s known and as enduring, all cognitive objects are equal. They are different in the way that they are unified. Anything that is one thing, must have unity of a kind; what is special to the aesthetic object is its indivisible unity.

There are only two ways, fundamentally, that unities can be distinguished—those in which the parts when separately taken remain unaltered, and those in which they do not. Those of the first kind make up the class of scientific objects, those of the second, that of aesthetic objects. No third class seems possible, except the mixture of the two. Those which are not mixed represent the objects of pure science and pure aesthetics. In perfect purity, they do not exist, but knowledge becomes pure to the extent that one or other of these knowledge types controls the situation. They will have to be thoroughly discussed even if it costs something in the way of tedium, for only so can any measure of intelligibility be brought into aesthetics.

A cognitive object is of the scientific type when it is composed of two parts which stand to each other in such a relation that one refers to the other, and adds some information concerning it. If we say that A is A, we say nothing at all, unless the statement is not true. In order that there should be a meaning we would have to add a difference. If we said that A in this place is A in that place, we would be asserting an identity in a context of difference, and therefore we should really be saying something. When we say that a horse is an ungulate mammal, we are saying that the familiar animal that draws carts and bears riders on its back is a mammal and has one toe on each foot. We are adding nothing to the horse which already had its mammae, if a female, and its four single toes, but we are possibly adding to someone's knowledge who did not know that a horse was a mammal or an ungulate. The most elaborate of scientific generalisations is nothing more than a statement of this kind. In every case the scientific object is a propositional object, expressed or implied, in which there are at least two parts, related to each other in terms of mutual explanation.

In order to be a statement of the scientific type, the statement need not be demonstrable. It may be a wild guess, or an almost pure fantasy.

Much of science has at all times been of this sort. Of course it is only when statements are demonstrable that they can build up the structure of a progressive science, but science is science in form, even when it is bad science. Nothing is more misleading in definitions than to deny that something is the kind of thing it is when it is a bad specimen of its kind. That sort of assertion is cant, whether one says of a man born in America, of American parentage, but lacking in virtue, that he is not an American; or of a bad picture, that it is not art; or of bad reasoning, that it is not science. A thing is what it is, and what we say of knowledge about it must have regard to the norms of that knowledge. To mix in undeterminable personal valuation when we are ostensibly dealing with these norms, is to confuse things hopelessly. When one speaks of something one should intend that thing, unless one speaks figuratively. One should not confound terms of commendation, and terms of description.

Though science does not necessitate demonstrability, demonstrability applies especially to science. Demonstrability depends for its perfection upon enumeration or measurement. It is only when we can count or measure things that we can speak of them precisely. Accurate measurement depends upon instruments, for with instruments we can read the measurements upon a scale. Where neither enumeration nor accurate measurement is possible, the science is not exact. It may be good as far as it goes, but it only goes a limited way.

Generally people think that feelings have to do with the aesthetic world of interests, and not with science, but in a case like that which follows this is not true. The instance is important, because it will serve to take us across the interval that separates science and aesthetics.

Suppose we had no scales and that the only way we knew to find equality of weights was to take one thing on our right hands, and another on our left, and *feel* the equality or inequality. We are as definitely concerned with scientific fact as when we try to find out how much a light ray is deflected when it goes past the sun. The difference between what we commonly think is scientific testing, and such loose testing as this, depends upon the use in one case of created instruments, and on their absence in the other.

My special reason for using this illustration rather than one where there is merely unmeasured perception, is to bring in the idea of feeling. I want to show that feeling can enter as a factor in science when instrumental means are lacking to replace it. But the word *feeling* is not unambiguous, and therefore it will be necessary to distinguish the different kinds that can be noted in the given conditions.

There is, when we hold up the weights in the hands, a felt difference of quality. Besides this, there is the felt satisfaction in arriving at a solution. When we desire a solution, there is some discomfort which may be great or little according to circumstances, before we come to a settlement. For many psychologists the only admitted feelings are those of pleasure and displeasure, formerly called pleasure and pain, and in the present case pleasure and displeasure might be applied to the discomfort in uncertainty and the comfort in the solution.

There might possibly be another quality of satisfaction involved in the balancing of the weights. I might prefer that they should be equal or that they should not, and there would be pleasure or displeasure according as the expectation was or was not satisfied.

One hears a great deal about feeling in discussions of aesthetics, and a great deal about pleasure. The feelings are usually called emotions, and this word is used so loosely as to have no more meaning than to set apart conceptual thinking as non-emotional. Pleasurable feelings are commonly taken to be the essential ones in the description of aesthetic states, and beauty has even been called pleasure as the quality of a thing. But pleasure as the quality of a thing might be characteristic of any satisfactory result whatever. The beauty of four as the sum of two and two is its fitness as the answer to our question. The beauty of one horse's nose in front of another is the satisfactory solution of our expectation or of our bettor's hope. In all such cases there may be, and often is, a certain transformation of the thing through our satisfaction in its character. An object redounding to our advantage does not look exactly like the same object redounding to the advantage of another. There is no particular connection between pleasure as the quality of a thing and aesthetics. Pleasure can enter as the quality of a thing whenever we transform an object by seeing it as though it carried in itself the quality of feeling or the specific virtue that we desire for it.

Satisfaction in the presence of an object can be important for an aesthetic experience, but it is not the factor of primary importance. It does not characterise the experience but is one that may derive from it. To make aesthetic character depend upon the quality of satisfaction which the experience gives us is, in my opinion, to make the understanding of aesthetics impossible, and to render trivial a subject that is admittedly, and I think rightly, of the greatest importance.

Satisfaction is obviously important as a matter of practical interest. But it has nothing to do with our present subject, which is the defining of objects. Feelings enter into this, but feeling is more analogous to the felt character of the weights in the hand. But even this does not explain how feelings are related to aesthetics, and some other things still require discussion before we can go more deeply into the matter. At present I shall content myself with affirming my belief that aesthetics has to do with knowing, and with knowing only. Its objects, which are enduring and unified, can be so only because they are intrinsically objects of knowledge. All other properties which they may have, and there are many, will be shown later to belong to applied and not to pure aesthetics. It is true that there is feeling which is intrinsic to aesthetic knowing, but it is a feeling that enters constructively into the object, and is not the feeling of satisfaction which derives from it.

The way in which a scientific object is known is radically different from the way in which an aesthetic object is known. In a chapter on Reality (Chapter XXI) I shall try to show that both ways are partial; that there is not certainly any single comprehensive way of *knowing* things; and that the importance of the aesthetic is the part it plays in making for our comprehensive action in our world. Therefore to distinguish as clearly and as realistically as possible between scientific and aesthetic ways of knowing, is centrally worthwhile.

The next two chapters will deal with scientific and aesthetic knowing, regarding first, the object, and second, the knower. I have said something of the unification that occurs in science. The way that the aesthetic object is unified will have to be set forth at length. But, of course, the way that this takes place depends upon the nature of the knower. Scientific and aesthetic knowers are very different, and the subject of aesthetics cannot be made clear unless acquaintance with them is made.

To end this chapter I shall try to make clear by a very simple instance that the aesthetic object is essentially a cognitive object. Let anyone look at anything that lies before him on the table, or is anywhere in the room, or outside the window. Let him have it clear in mind that he is to prevent his attention from becoming inventorial. Let him, that is, look at the things before him, no matter how numerous, as a single object and without making a list. Let him persist in doing this for a while without allowing his mind to wander, or to become hypnotised. To get this result he must let his eyes move freely without strain, passing from one object to another in order to keep them together, not to separate them. If he succeeds in doing this, he will find what is before him to be a picture. In a later chapter this kind of effort will be gone into more thoroughly, and it will be shown how one can make not only pictures but good pictures. Here it is sufficient to point out that getting to know what is before one, in a certain way, is picture making. This is in essence what aesthetic activity amounts to. It will need a good deal of rather dull analysis to show, in detail, just what happens.

IX. Propositions and Symbols

THE OBJECT CREATED IN scientific seeing is often said to be abstract. There are at least two things that can be meant by abstraction, and these are of confused. They must be clearly distinguished.

The kind of abstraction that is peculiar to science among knowledge forms, requires that all its propositions should be hypothetical. The things that we deal with in practical affairs are not the objects of pure science. They are the complex things we act on, and which act on us. But science cannot be content merely to act. Its business is to know. We can run away from a snake as a whole, but we can have knowledge about it only in detail. Science starts from something, a material thing or an idea, makes some partial assertion with regard to it, brings that in connection with some other thing, and asserts a relation between them. This assertion of relations makes the statement scientific. Whether the statement is true or not, nobody knows. All that one can know is that when the statement of relation has undergone development, and is returned to satisfactory contact with some things concerning which it has prophetically affirmed something, then the statement is called true. But it often happens that such statements continue to work, so far as possible detection goes, even when they are not true. This may be because the margin of error is too small, as with Newton's law when it applies to small velocities, or it may be because of less obvious reasons in more complex matters. All that we know or need concern ourselves with so far as science goes, is that propositions which are scientifically valid should at no point lead us practically astray when we re-encounter things. Science is abstract because its only concern is to assert that if A is thus so, and B is thus otherwise, that is, if the initial facts have been rightly observed, then an asserted relation between them is valid. To find out whether A and B are as they are asserted to be, is work for the discoverer and not the scientist. When the discovered object serves for scientific purposes we commonly speak of it as a scientific object. Of course the scientist does a great part of the discovering himself, but that fact does not invalidate the distinction.

That abstraction of this kind can be of use depends upon the doubling of the elements within the object of scientific knowledge, upon the fact that the whole object of scientific knowledge is always a proposition in which something is asserted to refer to something else—that the angles of a triangle are in some particular way related to two right angles, that the whale has a special connection with the group of mammals, and so on. It is this doubleness that makes logical development possible. If we start at some moment of actual contact with things, including possibly ideas, which have been discovered at some time by us or others, and assert relations, which in turn can be developed by applying to them further assertions of relations that are true of any facts—using, that is, logical forms—and if our eventual assertions of relations when applied in actual contact to the things toward which the whole process has been directed, are not inconsistent with the discovered nature of these things; we look on the whole process as good argument. Argument belongs to science and its particular type of abstraction. It does not belong to aesthetics.

There is another type of abstraction which belongs to aesthetics as well as to science—the abstraction from a whole. Science never deals with any actual whole. Anything, except possibly some logical ultimates—about them there is a difference of opinion—has more qualities than any single formula exhausts. It is like a star with points for many directions. Science at any moment selects someone or more among these, and develops the relations that can be grown between these and the points of another. An ideal science would eventually cover the whole universe with a network of relations, one that was so complete that the terms themselves would be necessitated by the relations, and everything that was possible would be inferable from the relations. In such a universe nothing would be left over for the discoverer, since everything could be inferred by the scientist. This kind of knowledge exists nowhere, not even, as I understand, in mathematics. Of no other subject is it true at all, though the mathematical physics of Einstein, Weyl, and Eddington, as I gather, makes the nearest approach to it.

Everywhere else discovery plays a large part. Science, for instance, cannot deal with cause, cannot explain it, though popularly that is thought to be its particular business. Causes are observed, and when they seem to be inferred, the inference is only by analogy from known cases. Science leads us to the discovery of many causes, but that is quite another matter. Popularly no discrimination is made between the processes of science and those of discovery. Science deals with atoms which do not interpenetrate, do not mix, do not change. They occupy positions in formulae, which relate themselves to things that have been, and to things that will be, discovered. But strictly speaking, all these structures of the scientific imagination cannot get away from their own hypothetical world, except to make their terminal references to the abstracted particulars which are found in things.

One of the consequences of this abstract character of science which denies it any relation to cause, is its incapacity to account for novelty, for any new thing happening in the world. William James was much concerned with this paradox that new things did happen, but that philosophy, which purported to be the science of sciences, could find no place for the happening. Later on it will become evident why these matters that seem rather far from what aesthetics is commonly supposed to be, have, of necessity, been taken into account. Science and aesthetics are the two parts of a greater whole, and neither one can be understood without the other.

All pure science is hypothetical and inferential. Discovery is an intrusion. All pure aesthetics is discovery, and inference, in aesthetics, is an intrusion. Inference depends upon the atomic nature of things, so that further relations may be developed. Discovery depends upon presented wholes, which may be found as such. Scientific systems are never absolutely pure. Actual aesthetic objects are never absolutely pure. Since science and aesthetics are so very different, abstraction in aesthetics must mean something very different from abstraction in science. The abstractions of science must serve to make comprehensive diagrams. The abstractions of aesthetics must serve to make concrete objects. The ultimate abstraction made by science from things, is the atom in its absolute sense. The ultimate abstraction made from things by aesthetics is the symbol.

When it is said that discovery does not belong to pure science, and that inference does not belong to pure aesthetics, and that in fact these subjects in their purity do not exist, it would be natural and easy to draw the conclusion that there is something of aesthetics in all science, and something of science in all aesthetics. But this conclusion, though obvious, would be false. Both of these are knowledge forms, and the conclusion so drawn assumes that the starting point for knowledge is itself an object of knowledge, that the process of knowing requires no other raw material than facts which are *known*. Yet this is no more true than that flour, yeast and water, are already bread. One can make bread of these but it has to be made. The analogy can be carried very far. We usually think of an operation in terms of the moment when it was begun, and the moment when it was finished. But this is not at all what happens. If we stop our bread-making at any time before the bread is finished it will not be bread. The intention to make the bread may well have had its own particular moment, but the making of the bread is a process of continually renewed beginnings. The law of inertia may apply to the intention, but it cannot apply to a process where there are, at every moment, changes in the direction of movement.

What applies to bread-making applies to knowing. Moments of attention are, as psychologists have seen, very short. The mind is like a lathe tool held against the bar which the worker is cutting. The tool is held there by a series of muscular contractions which succeed each other, and give an apparently continuous pressure. That they do not actually do so is made evident by the fact that the pressure has to be maintained. So it is with the mind in knowing. If the knowing interest is not kept up, the object becomes vague, or goes altogether from attention. Anyone who reads without interest can readily verify this. The mere thing with which we make and lose contact is not an object of knowledge, but an object to which we react. It is potentially all that we can make of it, in the way of knowledge, and so far as the two great divisions of the scientific and the aesthetic knowledge are concerned, it always keeps these potentialities of the mere thing. We are kept going by the recurrent stimulus of the thing. Therefore the inevitable impurities in science and aesthetics are due to the fact that the things to which we react always keep their primary inchoate character. They always remain raw material for the next stage. And it is this quality as initial raw material that keeps both science and aesthetics on the earth. So long as this condition persists neither the one or the other ever becomes pure form. In a later chapter we shall deal with *applied* science and with *applied* aesthetics, but the matter of that chapter will be essentially different from the matter of this paragraph. In those fields science and aesthetics do actually mix.

Before we take up the subject of the symbol we must give a thought once more to the primary abstraction that aesthetics makes from the whole of experience. Aesthetics concerns itself specifically with that which science leaves out. All that is specifically inventorial, that is atomic, that is hypothetical, does not belong to aesthetics. And this is true because the object for aesthetics is never doubled as it always is for science, but is always single, though its singleness may involve the utmost complexity.

The singleness of the object in aesthetics is the basis of one of the first rules of art, the rule of unity in variety. It means that the items which are taken from a whole of natural fact undergo change in becoming elements of an aesthetic whole, while those which are taken from a whole for science, being atomic, undergo no change. They merely are put elsewhere or into different surroundings. Of course where the thing for science is *created* by relations, like an equation, it cannot survive the sundering of those relations. It is like a Rupert's drop that is utterly disrupted by the slightest fracture. But where elements are separable at all, they are separable without change. The motions of the earth are modified by the presence of the sun, but the atomic fact of the earth's mass remains by this fact unaffected. It is not so with the note which the earth strikes in the music of the spheres. That would not remain the same if the sun ceased to sing. The music of the spheres is not for the attentive ear of God, a sum of parts, but their unison.

The singleness of the aesthetic fact is expressed in the symbol. There is, of course, a sense of the word symbol that is applicable to science as well as to aesthetics. That is the case when a symbol really means nothing more than a name. But the symbol for aesthetics means something very different from this.

For aesthetics the essential character of the symbol is variety in unity. The adequate explanation of this will be possible only when we have taken up the subject of the aesthetic knower, and have studied feeling. It is a commonplace that aesthetics has to do with quality, and quality is perception in relation to feeling. For the present I can deal with only so much of the meaning of symbols as can be understood when we consider the object only. For this purpose I return to where we left off—at abstraction.

To abstract in the sense in which the word has meaning for aesthetics, is to take a part of something met with in the world of experience, and then, without leaving it and passing on to something else, but instead, while still staying with it, to make it carry on to other things. We do this obviously when we repeat "Gather ye rosebuds while ye may." We are concerned with rosebuds only as they are fresh and delightful things, but we are still more interested in other things that are fresh and delightful. A symbol which has become a rubber stamp may get to be mere name. If rosebuds, for instance, meant delightful things without suggesting that they were themselves delightful, they would not be an aesthetic symbol but a mere caption.

This kind of abstraction from the whole of a presented thing is true not merely of objects as they are met with by the way, but as they are met with in the constructed aesthetic object, in a work of art, for instance. Every such expression involves certain relations existing among the actual points and lines, or words, or sounds, that are used. For instance in a picture, the surface of the canvas is covered with lines and coloured spaces. These indicate far more possible relations amongst each other than anyone can possibly get hold of at any instant. This is true even if the picture is not what is commonly called an abstract one. If I am looking for the first time at a picture in which are shown trees and personages and clouds in various colours and variously disposed, I see it first in terms of my recent seeing habits. Twenty years ago when I was specially obsessed by Cézanne's plastic presentations, I would have seen something very different from what I see today when those same plastic presentations are much less interesting to me than quantities of other things. One tries, even though unwittingly, to make of the picture a symbol of one's interests, just as the artist did when he painted it. If he is specially interested in "solidity" and paints a head, he tries to make it solid. He tries to make a statement not *about* solidity but *of* solidity. He does not try to make a wooden head but a solid flesh-and-blood head. A solidly painted head is the symbol of his interests just as a rosebud-gatherer is a symbol of Herrick's interest. If I take no particular interest in solidity and someone insists to me that the head is solid, I may answer that I quite well see it is, and what of it. People with a special interest in some quality have an innocent way of assuming that quality to be absolutely of special interest. They forget or are incapable of knowing that the abstraction which they make from all possible qualities that might in that situation come to expression, represents only a personal interest. They are interested in any sample of it, because it is a concrete symbol of a greater interest of theirs. People who do not have that interest do not note this quality in it, because they are not looking for that symbolic value. The habit of taking aesthetic objects absolutely and ignoring that they are the concrete symbols of interests, is the ground for critical dogmatism and fatuity. When one is simply looking at the object for one's present purposes there is no reason why one should be aware of this, but for purposes of critical reflection it is all-important that one should realise that every aesthetic object is a concrete symbol.

I said that when I first look at a picture I see it in terms of my recent seeing habits. If I am troubled with a certain inflexibility of spirit, or if I have reached the certitude that as I see things, things should be seen; it is not likely that further looking will cause me to take the picture otherwise than as I have taken it. But if through hard experience I have learned to know that my present seeing habits are just my present seeing habits, I may profitably look at it again. The things that I inventorially see are spots and lines, and more or less complete imitations of things otherwise existent. But for everything there is an environing field. This field is so large and various, and if one's spirit is flexible there is such constant streaming from it toward the present situation, that one may find, in fact I commonly do find, the picture changing to my vision. I started in by saying to it implicitly, "If the abstractions that you have made from the possibilities of meaning are not constitutive of a concrete symbol of what I at present demand, you are naught," and then I find myself implicitly saying to it, "What are your interests?" I start by having an opinion of it, and end by having thoughts about it. I begin with criticism, and end with apprehension. I begin with what it is not, and end with what it is. I begin with noting what it lacks, and end with noting what it gives. I now never think of a picture as bad unless I see how, without being made something else, it can be made better. Apart from that I never judge it, unless I am compelled to talk about it to someone who insists on an opinion.

I shall digress a little, before I finish this chapter, so that I may recall to the reader's attention certain things that have already been said but which are so contrary to the common habits of thinking in aesthetics that it is not likely that his mind effectively retains them. The most important of these things is the irrelevance of pleasure as a specific and peculiar factor. This is not the most important thing in point of principle, but it is very important in point of practice. The matter can come to exhaustive treatment only when applied aesthetics is our theme, but since this way of thinking is the greatest obstacle to taking the aesthetic object as a cognitive object, it must be recalled from time to time. People have in general not the least idea how little they see aesthetically. They are so quick to criticise if they are checked, or to wallow if they are not, that the object hardly serves for more than to start them off in one or other of these directions. But under these conditions the object itself is really trivial, and the results are unimportant so far as they are specially connected with aesthetic experience. We quite commonly criticise, for most gossip is criticism, and most of the comment that we make on any matter. And as for pleasure, we take that where we may, and, in fact, find plentiful occasion. If the aesthetic experience has exceptional value it cannot be for what it contributes to these ends, for in respect of these it has no exceptional position. It has, however, an exceptional position as the experience of a peculiar cognitive object, and this object is a symbol, the symbol of an interest.

I said above that the object of criticism or of pleasure is rendered trivial if the really important value is the critical activity, or the pleasurable feeling. It is equally true that the object cannot get importance merely by becoming a symbol. After all, a symbol, even at its best, is just a symbol. But if it is the symbol of something important which can be concretely symbolised only by such a symbol, then it becomes important as the unique expression of something important. That is my claim for the aesthetic symbol, and that is the reason why I think it worthwhile writing a book about aesthetics. The development of this theme comes in the next chapter and to avoid unnecessary repetition I shall leave it now. It is sufficient for the moment to have recalled the central topic, and I can now take up again the symbol in itself.

The symbol of science is different from the symbol of aesthetics, especially in this that the scientific symbol, being merely a name, is external to what it symbolises, whereas the symbol of aesthetics is internal to what it symbolises. The symbol in aesthetics is not a label, but a sample. It is a partial presentation that means more or less sufficiently the kind of thing that it refers to. But a thing which is a sample and not a name, can never be in all ways precise. A sample of cheese can tell you what the cheese is like, but it cannot tell you how much there is of it. Names are, on the whole, more satisfactory on condition that the thing named is invariable, and is well known. This is what happens in the purer science, in mathematics for instance. Names can here be built up into so complete a structure as practically to cover the whole field. But that can never happen with the aesthetic symbol. Two symbols cannot be placed edge to edge because they have no edges. An aesthetic symbol can have an approximately determined centre, but it cannot have an even approximately determined contour. Each symbol is a concreted abstract from the kind of interest to which it refers; it derives from and points toward the indeterminate but comprehensive ocean of significance that relations of the given kind imply; but no group of symbols exhausts the ocean as a whole, nor wholly exhausts any particular drop of it.

The character of the aesthetic symbol justifies one in saying that an artist always means what he says but never says what he means. The scientist tries to make his statements as clear as possible. He uses symbols—names—labels—which are competently understood only if we know exactly what they mean. A pound, a metre, lead, mass, acceleration—all these terms are quite particular. Science concerns itself with atoms in relation. Aesthetics concerns itself with relations which atoms point toward. The artist uses his atomic details, his lines and spots and represented objects, his words and tones, to express meanings that go beyond, and sometimes quite aside from, the obviously explicit meanings of the details themselves. Therefore he does not say what he means, although he means what he says.

X. The Knower

SINCE AESTHETICS HAS TO do with knowing, knowledge about it must concern itself with two factors—the object and the knower. So far we have had to do mostly with the object, and now we shall turn to the knower. Since, furthermore, there must be adequate discrimination between the knower in science and the knower in aesthetics, it will be important to have such an understanding of knowing as will make the discrimination rather fundamental, at least for practice.

I shall define knowing as *awareness in terms of two co-ordinates.* This definition will, I think, serve our purposes.

To show what can be meant by awareness in terms of two co-ordinates, I shall take an instance where awareness come of seeing on one line only. Suppose a person to be pursuing an animal, a fox. We shall a suppose him to be interested in getting to know the animal, but to be prevented from getting to know it in terms of relations, or of doing anything except to take on the animal directly. If he thinks of it as brown, or running, or as anything whatever except as what-is-there, he is complicating the cognitive situation. He is not taking it directly, but is seeing it through the concept brown, or running, or whatever.

If the approach to the animal by any roundabout method is avoided, there remain two possibilities—either the response to a stimulus as when a kitten jumps at whatever moves undangerously; or an assimilation to the animal through an imaginative identification with it. I do not mean to say that this is a more primitive way of knowing, a kind of precognitive state, though it is unquestionably more used by children and by primitive minds than by mature men of science. It is not my purpose anywhere in this book to speculate about origins. Practically it will be found, I think, that apprehending anything, while excluding all the means of knowing, other than the present thing in its completeness, makes necessary an apprehension through being it. We know it, in so far as we are it.

This is commonly the mind's state in the day-dream or revery. One often does something like it in actual planning, when one imagines oneself in a situation, and sees from there, what needs to be done. But in such instances there is more displacement than identification. In the day-dream there is identification, because one makes oneself one with the whole of another situation. One is the hero-being-heroic, the rich-man-enjoying-his-riches, the beautiful-woman-being-adored. It is often believed that this kind of thing is what aesthetic experience should be. But if this were so, the aesthetic experience would be either delusive or pernicious. In truth this has no more to do with aesthetics than with science, although there are good reasons, which will later appear, why it should seem to be more closely connected.

There is one kind of single-track approach that is supposed to have, and may have, a real value greater than that of the day-dream. There is, perhaps, a valid mystical experience. Its possible validity can be understood if we compare mysticism and mathematics. Mathematics is almost pure science, because inference makes so large a part, and discovery so small a part, of it. The more that mathematics is made arithmetical, the more this is true. But in the other sciences, dependence on inference is misleading. There was, for instance, a moment in the course of modern philosophy when nature-philosophers were popular. Evolution of a pre-Darwinian kind was current. Philosophers thought that by combining the notion of evolution and a few facts about living things and their environment, the history of life in all its forms could be written offhand. A number of these histories were written, but they did not last. The sciences of nature depend on a judicious mixture of inference and discovery, and an overthrow of the balance in either direction will turn the science toward the arid, or the fantastic.

What inference does for science, direct inner experience does for mysticism. The mystic does not learn by observation or discovery but by identification. He gives an accurate account of the world-beyond-world only as he is it. The mystics' descriptions of that world are much too various, and too much contaminated by their dwelling-places in this world, to give us confidence. They remind one of the nature faker. The faker writes the autobiography of the fox, the horse, the lion, or the crow, but if we are critical we believe so much as rests on observation, and take the rest as possible fiction. There are too many differences between man and these animals, and we cannot easily believe that the man's impressions authentically translate the animal's. If the nature faker were content to write the autobiography of an amoeba, or even of an oyster, the story would be more plausible. That of a primitive protoplast would be the most plausible of all. The nearer one comes to the bare fact of vegetative existence where there is nothing to tell, the more truth there would be in the tale. At the level where they are just alive, the amoeba and the man are probably at one.

What is true of the nature faker is true of the mystic. The single approach of identification can give sure knowledge only of that which is common. Being would be magnificently shared in common, if there is a way of experiencing pure being. If there is not, the mystic is always something of a faker. If there is, the experience cannot be reported. Authentic knowing along a single line may authorise some further guessing, but it permits no accurate testimony regarding that which lies beyond the participated-in reality.

We can turn now to knowledge by co-ordinates. One of the co-ordinates is obviously given. It is the line that we have already referred to, along which a thing is noted. The nature of the thing has nothing to do with the distinction in ways of knowing, that we are to be concerned with. Whether it is a brass candlestick on the mantelpiece, or the memory of the candlestick, or an idea of a candlestick, is indifferent. In some sense the thing is before me. What the other co-ordinate is, will determine what kind of an object the thing turns into, and what kind of knowledge we shall have.

When Descartes discovered analytic geometry, he did over, and developed further, that which nature had done when it invented binocular vision. He isolated a point by getting two converging lines to cross upon it. The millions of diagrams that every year are made to trace the curves of everything imaginable, are applications of this process. The kind of knowledge that we get depends on the derivation of the co-ordinates. For Descartes, the important thing was the length of the lines that marked the point. For a general theory of knowledge, the important thing is the field that the second co-ordinate traverses. By defining the field, we shall be able to distinguish the two great groups of objects—those which are compound, and those which are complex; the objects of science, and the objects of aesthetics.

The fact that the object of science is always compound, that is, always consists of a proposition with two terms, makes it possible to approach either term through the other. If we look directly at A, we can at the same time look at it indirectly through B. So for the reverse direction. We see the compound object as one, because our other co-ordinate always passes through the other term. The whale is a mammal. Mammalian characters are illustrated by the whale. The scientific object is both made and made manifest, by the co-ordinates. This is so obvious in the case of science with its compound object, that we can leave it with these few words. The case of aesthetics is more difficult.

The aesthetic object is complex but single. We see it before us, but how has it come to be there, and how do we make acquaintance with it?

It is obvious that people might see whales nursing their young for a long time, without suspecting them of being mammals. Mere similarity in some habit would not necessarily suggest putting whales and cows so close together. To see things together when the relation is not an inference from what is already known, means discovery. Propositions, when they do not come into existence inferentially, must be invented. These relations are invented, because seeing one of the things by using a co-ordinate drawn through the other, will make the one better known than it was before. Increase of knowledge is here an obvious motive. The question for aesthetics is—through what is the other co-ordinate drawn, and what is the motive for drawing it? If aesthetics is a way of knowing, the knower must be a person who uses that co-ordinate.

The other co-ordinate is drawn through the *self*, and the motive is *to use the self as an object of cognitive experience*. People to no small extent appreciate themselves, and in aesthetic experience they find their selves projected, and available to observation. The grounds of acceptance or rejection are personal grounds, for the aesthetic object exists only by virtue of the personal relation.

Since the aesthetic object is constituted by, and is made known through, the self, we cannot possibly know much about aesthetics unless we understand the self. But if the definition we have given of knowledge is correct, we should be able to find out something that is worth knowing about the self, by drawing the appropriate co-ordinate. This can be done. The self can be made known *through another knower, because it has existence only as a social product.* The self is made where the individual cuts across the line of the community. The self is found at this intersection. It is at this intersection only, that it can be known.

One's self is what oneself would be known-as, if one knew oneself. It is the whole of one's personal means as these have been forged upon the anvil of the world. I speak of it as a self, though so to speak is flattery. At best it is an armoury, a collection of tools, a closetful of chemicals. It is the instrument by which the individual advances beyond the stage of his primitive existence. It is what makes the body to become a mind, or if the mind has been neutrally given, it makes the mind particular. The self is the grouping of the feelings into more or less stable wholes. Feeling, as we said in an earlier chapter, differs from seeing in that it is vague. The more or less of unity in the self is due to the fact that feelings of response, whether to the outer world of matter, the inner world of matter, or the world of ideas, are vague, without clear centres or sharp edges, and can therefore fuse and unify themselves. Feelings of position and poise, feelings about one's desires and their consummation, feelings about one's loves and fears, all this kind of thing enters into the constitution of the self.

Psychologists commonly study knowing as a process directed outwards, and have generally ignored the process of being known. This seems to me an omission that makes the constitution, and the knowledge, of the self, inexplicable. The self is made exactly where the lines of knowing and being-known cross each other. Explicit knowledge of it is possible only to the extent that there is realised the need of seeking it at this intersection. If people really stood outside each other and could not know themselves as others know them, they would not be able to understand themselves or each other, except in so far as they dealt with things existing in the world of atomic objects. The world would be a common world only in so far as two and two make four. But people are parts of a social world. They *do* see themselves as others see them. Of course, others do not all see them alike, and they make choice, among the views that others have of them, of those views which are most consonant with their own desires. Not literally. They are not free to do that. They are partially aware of how they look to those who regard them none too favourably. They cannot get away entirely from condemnation, and the resulting impression is usually complicated and confused. It is often full of conflict. The important thing that we must remember, is that we see ourselves as others see us; that we see ourselves only because others see us; that we see ourselves because we are members of society, and share in the knowledge that its members in common possess. Each one arranges this knowledge as far as possible to suit himself, and so it happens that no one sees himself exactly as anyone else sees him. But neither do two others see him exactly in the same way. However, if the man is not mad or defective, there enters into the knowledge of him by others, nothing that is essentially impossible to his knowledge of himself. It is inconvenient for him to know certain things, and inconvenience often amounts to virtual impossibility.

The self is, then, an object, brought to being by the intersection of lines running from the individual looking out, and the individual looking in. The explicit knowledge of the self is made possible by the same method. One's self, to repeat a formula, is what oneself would be known-as if one knew oneself, and one can come to know one's self very well if one will follow out as far as possible, and explicitly, the process by which the self gets to be made. This would mean to know oneself in social terms, and of course, society includes both oneself and others.

The subject of the self is not exhausted, but we have said enough for our present purpose, which is to find the field through which the second co-ordinate is drawn for the purposes of aesthetic knowing. We must next consider how in practice the line is drawn.

The aesthetic object is always complex, even if it is, in a particular instance, very little complicated. It must, at the least, be perceptible, and therefore be relieved against other things. The other things may exist only in memory. If I see a yellow spot in the undifferentiated expanse of a yellow wall, that spot of yellow is positively existent for me only because the yellow stands out against other colours, that are not really present. I have known yellow in distinction from other colours at previous times, and this foreknowledge makes possible the knowledge of this moment. This kind of aesthetic object is the simplest that can be conceived. Most kinds are more complicated in their immediate presentation. Differences are usual in the actually presented object.

I pointed out before how for science, objects that do not otherwise exist are made from existent things, by the abstraction of those properties of the things, that can be interestingly related to properties in other things. In some cases further relations expressed in propositions, can be developed inferentially, and in some cases they can be developed only by discovery. The terms get their meaning in the propositions, when they are seen through the co-ordinate of the other term.

The aesthetic object also consists of properties abstracted from things. A picture hangs before me showing different kinds of trees, a wall, a road, a house. One of the trees is a cypress. In this picture the cypress is for me only a tree and a spire of green. Only that, and nothing more. But I can easily recall a number of pictures where it is many other things besides this. It is very often a funereal symbol, and it is often a symbol of Italy. In those cases it strikes a very particular note. The picture before me was painted in Provence where there are cypresses, but where they are not characteristic of the landscape, as they are in Tuscany. The other trees in my picture dominate the landscape, not the cypress. If the same tree were transferred to other pictures that I know, I would abstract from the sum of presented qualities, others that would be relevant. Here I go no further than the shape and colour, and the tree-ness by virtue of which this particular tree is related to the rest of the trees, as it is not related to the wall or the house. Such is the meaning of abstraction, for the constitution of an aesthetic object. It applies even when two straight lines make up the whole of an aesthetic object, since so simple an object as two straight lines can be seen variously, as one relates the lines in one way or another.

If the aesthetic object is to be constituted by co-ordinates, of which one is drawn through the self, we must consider what the self does to effect abstraction of some particular properties, from all the properties which a thing as a whole suggests. The aesthetic object is made up of parts in unison, and therefore the line that passes through the self must in some way have the result of carrying the self into the object, of making it a part of the object. If the individual sees the object on one line only, he can know it through identification. If he sees it also through the self-co-ordinate, with special accent on the self, he subordinates the object to the self. If he sees it through the self-co-ordinate with the accent on the object, he subordinates the self to the object, and makes the object specifically aesthetic. The structural character of these relations must be made clear.

Feeling, because it is vague experience, makes possible the fusion of a multitude of perceptions, memories, ideas, into one. Since the objects are not clear, the impression that results, even when it is vivid, is rather unattached. But a floating feeling tends to trouble the person, who wants to have his feelings subdued to his demands. Therefore he attaches the feeling to one or another of the things to which it can be related. He makes of it a property either of an explicit self, or of something that is not self. I can say, "This chair is comfortable," or I can say, "Now I am comfortable." In the first case my feeling of comfort is made a property of the chair, and in the second, it is made a property of myself. In neither case am I stating the facts with analytic precision, but in both I am giving expression to a real experience. In the present instance it is not of great importance whether I take the matter in one way or the other, but the difference in these ways of taking them can in other cases have far-reaching consequences. In the instance of the first kind, the result tends toward the perception of aesthetic objects, and in the instance of the second kind, the tendency is toward the sentimental transformation of the object. There are extreme cases where only one or the other way of associating feelings and things is possible. Intangible bodily occurrences are known as feelings only, and on the other hand, we say that something is beautiful, and not that we feel beautiful in the presence of it. But there are intermediate stages, as when we look out on a great expanse of land or sea, and can say either that it is infinite, or that we feel ourselves to be infinite. The aesthetic unison means the transformation of the self in terms of the object, and sentimentality means the transformation of the object in terms of the self.

A one-line approach to the thing means knowledge through identification. Sentimentality means a turning in this direction. Instead of passing to the thing through the self, there is tendency to pass to the self through the thing, and as the self is not taken as a thing but as myself or oneself, the quality of objective character is lost. *I* am me, and *it* is me. The self becomes the gulf that swallows all distinctions. It is the wings with which I fly, and it is also the ocean in which I drown.

An interesting turn which this sentimentality takes is the "omnipotence of thought." In this case, thinking is itself seen through the co-ordinate of the self, is identified with the self, and loses the limitations of its rational character. Through the confusion of the individual or person with the self, the identification of the *I* with the *me*—the self comes to be taken as something other than the known product of a social interaction, and is held to be the individual in his active character. The free range of thought carries with it the ranging feeling of the self, and implies an equal competence of the person. Feeling, knowing, acting, are fused into a sentimental delusion of power, which is the "omnipotence of thought."

These matters are interesting, and it would be possible to go on indefinitely with them, but their further development does not belong to our subject. It is enough to have shown that the self is the mass of feelings, which takes the form of a mass because the individual feelings are vague, and do not point to their real objects, in fact, do not make objects in the sense in which I try, more or less consistently, to use the word. Because the self is indefinite, being made up of feelings that are indefinite, it easily assumes various forms, each of which seems for the moment, complete. When it is brought into relation with other things, the characteristic consequences follow from the self's indeterminateness. The two terms of a scientific relation are both definite. Therefore either term can be seen through the other without it undergoing change. But the indefiniteness of the self makes it difficult to relate it to a thing and still to keep it distinct. It acts like a semi-transparent medium through which the thing is seen, whereupon the thing ceases to be that thing, and becomes an aesthetic object. The medium is like a selective screen which abstracts from the whole of the thing those properties that are appropriate to its present state, and it tends to treat the thing as though it were, in reality, identical with the object that has been made by the selective action. The case is exactly analogous to ordinary vision, when we see a distant object through a transforming atmosphere, and ignore that we see the atmosphere. The atmosphere is like the self in that we do not use it, except when something else is going on, but really, we notice its effective consequences almost all the time, because something is almost always going on. The scientist tries to see in an atmosphereless world, and therefore thinks in terms of atoms, and not in terms of vision, but the aesthetic whole cannot be atomised, therefore the atmosphere of self is an integral part of the aesthetic object.

It is as reasonable to accept the aesthetic creation for its given values, as it is reasonable to accept the rainbow. But it is as unreasonable to interpret it in terms that do not belong to it, as it would be to dig for colours in the rainbow. Mysticism is sentimentality, taken seriously. Sentimentality is frivolous mysticism. If the basic identification of mysticism is valid, then the basic identification of sentimentality is also valid. But there is little ground for believing in either, except possibly on that deep level where all things are one. The truth of mysticism, if there is truth, is ineffable. In aesthetics there is no truth, but there is fact, and fact may be, and is, as important as truth.

XI. The Aesthetic Symbol

IN THE LAST CHAPTER the symbol was hardly mentioned, although in the preceding one I had said that the ultimate unit of aesthetics was the symbol. The nature of the aesthetic symbol must be our next subject.

A symbol, it was said, is for aesthetics, not a name but a sample. Therefore to know what the symbol can refer to, we must know the nature of the referred-to things. From what has been said it is clear that these things involve the self, and the self has been defined as the more or less knowable point of intersection between an individual and others, that is, the intersection of the individual and the community. The things that we are concerned with are distributed from this point. It is the market-place for feeling in its objectifiable form.

Some feelings are well-known, and some are not. The most pervasive and the best known are the feelings of *me*, and of *you*, and of *you-with-me*, and of *you-against-me*. These are the most commonly employed of all the selective screens in the world, and they are employed with the greatest intensity of interest. It is easy to say a lot about these feelings, but the poets and novelists have spent upon them so lavishly the richness of their word treasures, that everyone's attention has been sufficiently called to them. To name them here is all that is needed.

The feeling of *mine*, is equally important, but it is somewhat less reputable. It is the greatest of the feelings in the world of action, but it is rather kept down in the world of cognitive events. The desire for possession is more attractive as an idea, when it looks like something else. The self is specially devoted to appearance, and since feelings are essentially vague, it is easy for the self to seem like what it isn't. It is largely made up that way.

The self has no reality except in terms of direct or indirect knowledge. In fact since it is created and is known through the co-ordinates of *I* and *others*, it cannot come into effect otherwise than in terms of a certain publicity. I have already said that each person is not merely an individual but a community. Members of the community of the person, are often as hostile to each other as any outsider possibly could be. A man has no more the desire to know himself, than the desire to be known by others. The single member of the home community prefers the single line knowledge which means identification, with a large field of unconsciousness, to the co-ordinate knowledge gotten through the other members of the community. The unconscious, which is the master-word in the jargon of our day, is that portion of his self which a man can only treat, or which he prefers to treat, in terms of identification rather than in terms of co-ordinates. He would rather see with it than know it. The unconscious, in the technical Freudian sense, is not the cause of anything, except stoppages and loops. We either cannot go on at all, and mill like crowded cattle, or else we go round.

The self is largely a conventional thing. What we may admittedly know it as, is determined almost entirely by the habitual thought of the society in which the individual lives. It is especially for such characters of the self as *me, you, mine*, that it is rigorous in its scope of admitted attitudes. But there are other characters in respect of which the self is relatively open, or rather there are characters that are too elementary to be quite determined by any rule of conduct. Such are feelings of poise, rhythm, mass, and these are feelings of the greatest importance for aesthetics.

Man is a bilateral biped, and must always recover his disturbed equilibrium or fall. Therefore symmetry, or an asymmetrical recovery of balance, is essential to him. A four-footed animal would never, in all probability, have developed the arts. His equilibrium is too stable. Perhaps that is the reason that birds in their courtships develop what among animals comes nearest to a dance. A great deal will have to be said later about poise and rhythm; here it is necessary only to point to the fact that these characters are deep-seated in the self, and that they come to expression in all the arts, in forms that are quite readily taken on by most persons. Nothing is easier than to acquire an unfamiliar rhythm unless one is hardened in routine, or has moral objection to it. Of this an instance is the quick accommodation to new fashions. And except in cases of strait-laced protestation, or caste tradition, the objections are not very effectual. Rhythm and poise are not usual occasions for repression, though limitations in their exercise often result from repression.

It is of course not my intention to make an inventory of self-feelings, but I shall mention a few others of diverse character in order to make clear the meaning of the self.

The most interesting discovery of behaviourist psychology, for me, is the fundamental character of the fear of falling. It is quite possibly the feeling that enters most importantly into rhythm, which is the satisfaction in recovery from an incipient fall. Nothing is more unpleasant than a fall which does not promise recovery, but a fall which does, holds within itself the essential quality of excitement. The fear of falling is also to be related to the sense of reality, which is essentially the sense of support. Superficial critics have a way of making fun of people who attach importance to the felt reality of objects in art, and doubtless the notion is not always applied profoundly. But at bottom the people who want things to be real are more nearly right than most of their critics. All men demand reality, and these very critics cling as fervently to their trumpery aesthetics, as the victims of their castigations cling to their trumpery art. All men demand reality, and the secret of a sane life is to find the ultimate reliance that promises no more than it can perform. That is the meaning of an ultimate reliance on truth.

Man is the fore-and-after-looking animal, and so has come to think much of beginnings and ends, and of that which has neither beginning nor end. Alpha and Omega, and the cycle of eternity, are among his most valued inventions. His sense of personal importance is enormously stimulated by these ideas and their corresponding feelings, and the symbols that he has invented for them are almost as numerous as the symbols of love and fear.

Man is a wanderer on the earth, but he gets tired. The desire for home and mother are strong within him, and he feels their worth both as that from which he has come, and as that to which he is going. The feeling is different from that of beginning and end. It is more the Antaeus feeling, the touch of earth which nourishes and refreshes. Mother earth, the feeder and restorer, is its appropriate symbol. There are innumerable expressions of the earth's abundance, and the fatness thereof.

It is time now to find out, if we can, what precisely a symbol is.

I pointed out how for an absolute science, the terms reduce to ultimate abstractness. They become, analogously to the ether of nineteenth-century physics, the medium by virtue of which relations exist. But in the actuality of science there are always discovered things from which suitable abstractions are made.

What happens in science happens similarly in aesthetics. The world of things that can serve the purposes of aesthetics is co-extensive with the things that man can perceive or conceive. But when they enter into this service they undergo abstraction. Aspects only of them are used, for their totality of aesthetic significance would be the totality of aesthetic relations into which they could enter. The selection of aspects is determined by interests whose practical regulators are the feelings. The thing which is seen through the co-ordinate of feeling, undergoes a reduction that is consonant with the dominant feeling. A pig in art may be essentially a living thing, essentially a massive thing, essentially a porker, or it may be a sacrificial animal at the Suovetaurilia. The idea of one or other of these things, turns the pig over to perception screened through the relevant feeling. The idea defines the object, but only vision can make it particular. But in fact, the object in art is never quite particular. An interest in a sacrificial pig as primary, refers the pig to the sacrificial occasion, and makes of it merely one term in a scientific proposition. This is that kind of a pig. The pig is aesthetically valid, however, because he carries with him the Suovetaurilian, that is the sacrificial, quality. But the expression of the spirit of sacrifice, even of a special sacrifice, is one that goes beyond this pig or any other. The pig is a definite quantity, but the feeling is a definite quality. The pig is the sample expression of the qualitative character of the feeling. Most feelings that can come to expression can be represented by innumerable samples, and therefore, poets often pile metaphor on metaphor, just as painters, for the expression of a certain quality of form, will take as a model anyone of a thousand suitable things. In all these cases, the quantitatively limited expression is the sample, the symbol of a qualitatively unlimited feeling. Any aesthetic expression is such a sample or symbol. Therefore the symbol is the unit of aesthetics.

There is a group of modern artists who have consciously developed an abstract art. But in fact, there never was an art that was not abstract. There is no expression that is not abstract except what is an actual duplication. To like a picture because something represented in it looks like something outside it is to destroy the individuality of the picture, and make it part of a larger whole which is not an aesthetic whole. But to like a picture of something because it feels real, is to make abstraction of one of the most significant of feelings. The abstractionists in art are simple-minded people who by mistake have wandered into the world of science. They remind me of a friend who used to say, "If perfection is good, more perfection is better." They might say, if they knew enough to say it, "If abstraction is good, the thinner the abstraction the better." Science which lives on relations gets fat by thinning its abstractions. But aesthetics which lives on feelings, gets fat by fattening its abstractions. Propositions and symbols, like Crabbed Age and Youth, cannot live together, at least not on terms of perfect equality, nor does the same diet suit them. To each one that which is good for him, applies to science and aesthetics as well as to other things. To be naïvely scientific is not to be aesthetic but is only to be confused, and of this confusion almost all that is commonly said about aesthetics is a shining example.

XII. Distortion

DISTORTION IN ART HAS in recent years come to be seen as an important matter. Although we had long been familiar with distortion in caricature, in grotesques, and in decorative and stylistic painting, we did not think it otherwise important. The distortion that had occurred to a greater or less extent in the art of all times was taken to be exaggeration, and was accounted something abnormal and not essentially important. But since Cézanne, it has become evident that distortion has some important relation to art, that it is something other than exaggeration, and that possibly it may be something essential.

In this chapter I shall consider it in a very large way. It is not the distortion that is found in modern art that is my theme, for that is only a special case of the distortion that is found in all art, and more than that, in all aesthetic experience whatever. This distortion depends upon the changes that the thing undergoes in the process of becoming an aesthetic object. Distortion in aesthetics is due to the fact that abstractions from the thing are made, and seen, through the medium of the self. What the nature of the distortion is to be, depends upon the interest which the self has to satisfy.

We have barely brought in the interests so far, and this is not exactly the place where the discussion of them belongs, but since something must be said, it may as well be said now.

Interests are the properties of the individual, as feelings are of the self. As always in this book, I am concerned with questions of practice, and the definitions themselves are only practical conveniences. It is therefore sufficient to stress interest as that property of the individual, which determines the selective action of the self. Interest is the emergence of impulse into the field of action. The remoter causes may be instinctive, or they may be secretions, or any other disturbances of an existing state of tranquillity; for our purposes their import is—that the individual is impelled to do something. The particular something that we are considering is the aesthetic activity. The individual is interested in some scene or in some group of resurgent ideas, which he proposes to make real for seeing.

These things, even as they first arise in his mind, are affected by the self. The self is not only a screen through which things are aesthetically perceived, but it is a screen also in that other sense, of being that through which things are selected for presentation to view. Interests often call for things that are incompatible with the conservation of the self. Sometimes the self can screen them out entirely, but more often it will arrange for their more discrete appearance, and will permit them an actual though disguised presentation on the stage.

The aesthetic object is a whole made up of parts which are, inventorially considered, separate. These are, to some extent, arranged without reference to the peculiar prejudices of the self. If there are to be trees in a picture, these will be put right side up rather than standing on their tops, because that way of placing trees satisfies our sense of rational order. But as soon as we get away from any question of rational order, something else must be appealed to, and that is feeling. When feeling intervenes there intervenes that which for rational order is caprice. Caprice in this sense need not mean caprice in the usual sense. It means only that feeling is jury and judge. The aesthetic interest in science is, for instance, the self's acceptance of a rational order. It may insist upon the science being very pure. But it cannot be held to this. As soon as it tires of science in its crystal purity it flushes it with rainbow colours, or throws it aside for something more attractive. The acceptance like the rejection of the rational order is capricious.

Very little of aesthetic activity is concerned with pure rational order. Man always must have order in his experience, for without order he could make no adjustment to his environment, but a rational order is too exigent for his demands. Besides that, rational order when it gets beyond the obvious and apparent, demands understanding, and for the things that most appeal to men, our knowledge of the rational order is very slight. Therefore in respect of most of that which interests him, he looks for an aesthetic rather than a rational order, and when he has found one that satisfies the self, he assumes the rationality without pressing, the enquiry. He creates through the self a possibility of knowledge, which later, through the self he discovers as knowledge, and he is delighted to find how perfectly knowledge is adapted to his capacities and to his nature. This is the intuition by virtue of which everyone is right, and everybody else is wrong.

Distortion for a theory of aesthetics does not necessarily imply a neglect of the rational order. It is the result of a different way of taking the material. There hangs in the next room the picture of a woman sewing. The action of pushing the needle through the cloth is beautifully rendered. From the point of view of science the finger of one sewing occupies successive points at successive moments, but in this picture the finger is at all moments where it is and where it isn't. On the canvas it occupies a definite place, but there is so much of suggested movement that when I look at the hand I do not see it confined to that or any other spot. It belongs definitely in the composition, but the composition is a dynamic one and therefore any element of that composition is not only where it is inventorially to be found, but is also anywhere where it works. The distortion which is of the essence of aesthetic expression is the distortion that makes effective such action at a distance. It produces what we call the unity of the work of art. No aesthetic expression is without it. Aesthetic unity can be obtained only by breaking through the defined contours of the inventorial object, and through effecting a fusion of the content. Every aesthetic expression is dynamic, and therefore involves distortion.

There is such a thing as distortion in science as well as in aesthetics, but that is a very different kind of thing. The self is concerned essentially in science only to the extent that there is a felt interest in knowledge—curiosity, it is of called—which directs the individual towards the processes of science. Of course there are personal conditions of this direction of interest, but the important thing is that the self should not pervade the result. Through the self is brought about the contact between the individual and the things, but the scientific object into which the self enters as a factor, is a scientific object which has been corrupted. The scientific object is complete in itself because of its double nature. It involves abstraction but not distortion. The aesthetic object being single depends upon the self, whose purposes bring about a distortion of the naturalistic, atomistic, character of the individual thing which enters into the composition of the aesthetic object.

Both the scientific and the aesthetic objects are cognitive objects, but there is this important difference that for the scientific object knowing is a purpose, an interest, while for the aesthetic object it is not. For science we want to know what something is, and to get this result we relate it to something else. But in aesthetics we want the object to serve the ends of the self, and in the course of satisfying this purpose we create a cognitive object. Often we satisfy the demands of the self with things that are known on the outskirts rather than in the focus of attention, and so we get the group of attenuated aesthetic objects which I shall call environmental, and which like decoration, or landscape gardening, serve to give a particular background and atmosphere. In this the knowledge of the object is minimised. But in the purer aesthetic experience at its maximal state, the object is intensely seen. We look at it however, not because we want to know that particular thing, but because it offers to the self a more or less adequate accommodation.

Distortion in aesthetics means simply that the things which are normally given in the course of practical experience, are selectively and in combination so treated as to satisfy an end of personal interest, and that in the course of this process their inventorial identity is respected, not for its own sake, but only in so far as the present attitudes of the self are compatible with it. By way of instance I recall what Matisse said to me several times, during that period when his pictures showed the most extreme distortions of natural forms. He said that he never began a picture without hoping that this time he would be able to carry it through without any distortion that would disturb the ordinary onlooker. But his greater demand was for certain qualities of plenitude and rhythm, and before he had managed to work up his inventorial items of human bodies and accessories to the conditions of his pictorial intention, they had been pulled entirely out of shape.

In Cézanne's pictures the conditions of distortion were the same. It was done on purpose but not, in childish language, intentionally on purpose. It happened once that a young painter asked me why Cézanne had distorted the dish in a certain picture that was before us. I told her to look at the picture, and to imagine the dish drawn as a proper ellipse. Of course she saw at once that this would not do. It would have been possible to have done a picture with the plate as a good ellipse, but in that case Cézanne would have had to make compensating distortions elsewhere. The kind of result that he was after could not be obtained by keeping a group of normally seen objects constant to their normal appearances. No aesthetic whole would allow of this completely, and Cézanne's less than some others. In a later chapter I shall try to put the reader in a position where he can see distortions growing before his very eyes, and then he will understand the matter better, but for the present we must look to other things.

The specific distortions that are the conditions of all aesthetic seeing, explain the education that makes the connoisseur. The average person in respect of art is like the average person in respect of manners. In his native conditions, and without paying especial attention, he naturally shows his personal characters of grace or stolidity, his ease or stiffness, or whatever. But the same person on his good behaviour, especially in unfamiliar conditions, may lose entirely his normality of conduct. This happens because he cannot establish a satisfactory relation between that which appears before him and his self. This could happen only if he were virtually unconscious of the peculiarities of the particular situation, and took his own way like a bull in a china shop; or if he were discriminatingly aware of it, and abstracted from the situation those elements with which he could deal, and tactfully avoided the rest. The connoisseur is in a similar position. Often he takes his self so absolutely as a standard that he can pronounce on anything, with no more preparation than to see the thing. He treats his habitual distortions as though they were norms. Sometimes he is sufficiently discriminating to know the measure of his self, and avoids pronouncements where he cannot penetrate. Others have less fixity of the self, and these can establish new relations with what they encounter. They not only recognise realms in which they are not competent, but they are ready to find their way, if possible, with as-yet-unheard-of conditions. Beware of the cultured person who is ready at a moment's notice to give a critical opinion on anything. Such a person is eminently competent to write a history of art, but he is good for little else. Sometimes he cannot even write a history of art. In that case he is usually a second-hand radical.

It is commonly said that in art the whole man comes to expression, but that science is concerned with abstractions. Art, as will be explained later, is never purely aesthetic—there is always involved something more than that—but even so, art does not appeal to the whole man. It does appeal to him as a whole but that is a different matter. The expression in aesthetics is always indeterminate, and therefore there is an indeterminate extent of the self involved. We know that in science there is a specific minimum which is the interest in knowing, and that its definite test is verification. But in aesthetics there is nothing verifiable. A change in opinion does not prove the previous one wrong, for often one comes back to it later. Another self-grouping seems to be involved. An aesthetic object is authentic if at any moment it is actually perceived as such. No picture is invalid, or definitely bad, if it represents any person's seeing. All we need to do is to put ourselves in that person's place, and we too will see it so. Perhaps we cannot do this, and certainly in many cases we do not want to, but that does not alter the facts. Either the self conditions, and enters into the object, or else it does not. As will have to be shown, there are some intrinsic conditions that measure the purity of a work of art as an aesthetic object, but I know of none that can determine whether one work or another fulfils these conditions, except a personal appreciation. Let any man stand by his appreciation, and he can with a perfectly good conscience defy the opinions of the most assured superiority. He is safe against all attack.

What the self involved in aesthetic experience at a particular moment is, one cannot say. It is the organised product of someone's past, modified by many adventitious, floating factors. Success or disappointment in some passing matter of business or love may have as much effect on any particular expression, as one's philosophy or religion. An ideal practitioner ought perhaps to ignore the passing event, but there is just as good a reason why he should ignore his philosophy and his religion. If we go behind the fact of what he at the moment is, we cannot stop short of demanding the normal man, the absolute human being. That demand is not worth entering on. To entertain it speculatively, would mean to have a competent philosophy. To entertain it practically, would mean to produce the man. The one enterprise is no more within the field of actual competence than the other. Therefore aesthetic distortion cannot be reduced to a system. It depends not only upon the changes imposed upon the inventorial things by the act of unifying them, but furthermore upon the irreducible idiosyncrasies of this man and that other, who does the unifying.

The mention of a possible standard of what is truly the aesthetically valid, other than the standard of personal projection or response, may be taken as an excuse to say something about ethics. Commonly we find a threefold division, the good, the true, and the beautiful—ethics, science, and aesthetics. A few words may justifiably be added to this chapter to explain why ethics has not been mentioned.

Ethics has not been mentioned, because it does not seem to me to be a special subject at all. It is an unintelligible mixture of science and aesthetics and prudential maxims. It has no subject matter except conduct in general. But the chapter on Reality (Chapter XXI) will try to show that conduct in general cannot be the subject matter of knowledge in any real sense. Conduct in general can be made intelligible only by a knowledge of things in general. Conduct as it has been is a matter of anthropology, and is a definitely historical-scientific subject. Conduct as the proper exercise of human faculty is the subject matter for the science of things in general, or philosophy. If ethics existed as a science it would be identical with philosophy, and the only understanding of conduct as a whole would be the understanding of the universe as a whole, at least of the universe as man can experience it. It is therefore quite reasonable that philosophers should be teachers of ethics. Spinoza's fundamental book is rightly called ethics, and Plato's or Hegel's or James's work was largely ethical.

The only reasonable objection one may have to concerning oneself seriously with the general subject of ethics is the same objection one may have to dealing seriously with philosophy—that there exists no method for handling it. I have for my part no prejudice against philosophy, or against ethics either, but I cannot, unfortunately, understand anything that I have ever read or heard on these subjects. Nothing holds. The authors do their best to tie hard knots in a rope of sand. In the old days of scholasticism it was thought possible to lay down definitions that were good once and for all, and after that to spin webs of dialectic from which an opponent could not escape. Today the definitions cause more trouble than the dialectic. No one's definitions are the same as anyone else's. All the boxing is shadow boxing, since the opponent is really no-one-knows-where. The lay-man who does not concern himself with niceties of definition, can have no idea of this. He knows that the results of philosophic study are not coercive, and he knows that they are unintelligible to him. If he read a little of the controversial and critical literature in the philosophical journals he would learn, perhaps to his surprise, that they understood by no one. Groups are often formed and philosophical platforms built, upon which young with co-operative ardour take their stand, but after a while they look on each other with suspicion. It never takes them very long to find out that the other fellow is not the friend they took him for, co-operation is chucked, and soon each one is in the ring battling for his own. What had happened, of course, was that each one had thought that the others agreed with *him*, and when he finds this is not so, he sadly says with Ophelia, "I was the more deceived." It's all quite funny though a little drear, but philosophers are, despite their lugubrious profession, a rather cheerful tribe. They nourish a perennial hope that something will turn up. Except perhaps for the poets, they are the greatest boosters on record, and though they are often down, they are never out. The less that anyone else believes in them, the more each believes in himself, and so each one is a tower of strength in his own desert land. His castle is impregnable, for nobody else can find it. In his solitude he has the best of company, for his only possible confidant is himself, and no doubt he understands himself best in his dreams.

I know, of course, that if any philosopher has read so far as this he will retort, "And you, are you not also a philosopher," since one of the philosopher's conventional beliefs is that to deny possession of a philosophy is already to assert one. However I am not guilty. I find that if I travel in some directions I can keep on going. I want to keep on going as long as I am alive because I am an animal. I want to do it intelligently because I am human. This, I should say, is nature, not philosophy. All the rest is ways and means. I want to go *somewhere* because going *nowhere* is unpleasant. I want to go where it seems *possible* to go, because to want to go where it seems *impossible* to go is to be unintelligent. I want to be as intelligent as may be in order to recognise possibilities. Since I am only human and since other people are also human, since to be intelligent is to be peculiarly and especially human, I cannot believe it probable that scientific or quasi-scientific knowledge which is not intelligible to anyone else, is effectively the product of intelligence. Therefore I prefer to discriminate between the doing which is knowing, and that which is not. It is perfectly consistent with my being human to do foolish things, because my human attribute of being intelligent is not perfected, nor is it unimpededly at work. But as long as I can see a difference between the folly of my action and the possibilities of my intelligence, I prefer to keep them separate. This is the same as saying that I may be foolish but I am not mad. I can recognise my folly. My foolish actions can be idiosyncratically personal, but my valid knowledge can hardly be so. The philosopher with unique knowledge that is unintelligible to everyone else is probably mad when the wind is north-northwest. He has not discriminated between scientific and aesthetic knowing, and takes what is not properly knowledge at all for one or other of these kinds. He is really confounding a course of action with a process of knowing. He takes his more or less foolish *action* to be *knowledge.*

XIII. Place, Direction, Interval, Tension

THE NEXT FEW CHAPTERS of this book will try to account for the specific characters of an aesthetic object, and to show how the aesthetic experience can be made effective. I believe that our habitual ways of dealing with art when we are serious about it, are absurd and futile, and that our current ideas about art education are worse than that—they are silly. This chapter deals with the elementary characters of an aesthetic object, and the following ones will try to show what aesthetic seeing actually is. After that it will be possible to make an accounting of art on the balance sheet of life.

The simplest character that a thing can have is that of just being there. The colour on the wall before me is just there. It is a uniform yellow tone, which does not hold my eye to any part of it. To move from one part of it to another is not to modify the nature of the experience, for nothing happens with the change except the felt change itself, and that is not felt as related to the yellow of the wall, but to other conditions that enable us to mark a change in spatial positions.

What is true of a perceived yellow is equally true of an imagined yellow, or a conceived yellowness, or of anything else which has only one distinguishing character. Such are simple sights, or odours, or sounds like those of a tuning fork, or any concept of a simple thing. All these have the same characteristic attribute of simply being present to me.

The most elementary form, then, of an aesthetic object is that of a property which attracts interest and confers objectivity, but which has not within itself change, relation, proportion, balance, direction, or rhythm.

It is, of course, an obvious psychological fact that the thing could not be noticed at all if it were not different from or related to a difference in environing things. A universe that was all yellow might affect me physiologically by its yellowness, but I would never know it as yellow. When we speak of the pure blue of the sky, we imply knowledge of a blue that is impure. That blue may not be present when we look at the sky, but we see the pure blue that is present, through the impure blue that exists as a memory. It is not made explicit in the sight of the pure blue, but it determines the direction of the co-ordinate by means of which the present blue is made explicit. All this is too familiar to require more words.

The simplest alteration that a simple thing can undergo is to become part in a direction. The direction may be a line, a surface, a space; a transition to another tone or colour or timbre; a change in taste or temperature; the addition of words to each other to change the meaning; or it may be the idea of any of these things, or of anything whatever that can be seen or thought.

Mere direction has not very much meaning. It is like the child's eyes that follow a moving light, or like one's own eyes that cannot resist the movement of the after-images when one has been looking at the setting sun. There is movement, there is meaning, there is development, but without measure, without a constant direction, or determinate variation. Something more is necessary in order to give the object much value, and that thing is interval. Place, direction, interval, with tension, as the expression of the stress in change—in terms of these characters, the aesthetic object can get its full elaboration.

Interval as I shall use the term must be given a wide extension of meaning. It implies that whether the change is upward or downward, right or left, in space or in time, whether it refers to significance, or accents, or whatsoever can have the character of direction, that these changes come to have the quality of being felt as definite.

I say that the changes are felt as definite rather than that they are perceived as definite, because it is not the intervals that are perceived, but it is the object as a whole that is perceived with the intervals entering into the make-up of the whole. How the feelings may be thought of will need a few words.

We commonly say that we see a thing, hear a thing, smell a thing, when we do it distinctly, but we commonly use the word *feel* in reference to external objects when there is vagueness. We habitually say *feel* when we are concerned with touch where the confusion between feeling and the thing felt is very great. To feel in this sense means that there is something that we answer to, but which we cannot definitely establish. The indeterminate stimuli may be inside or outside the body, or may be merely in the mind. I have tried this experiment. I put a bottle on the table, noted clearly that it was *on* the table, and then I tried to do away with the bottle and the table, and leave only the onness. Of course I might have taken the onness as a concept, a general idea, but

I wanted a concrete onness and not a conceptual one. I found that as the bottle and the table dissolved away, their places were taken by felt stresses in the body, especially in the shoulders. Terms were needed for the relation of onness, and as the explicit terms were done away with, others less explicit took their places. But by a redirection of attention these could be made relatively clear. It is quite evident that direction, and even more obviously, intervals, need terms, and if the terms are not positively perceived the lack of them is made good by felt terms which may be indifferently inner or outer. It is often hard to tell which they are, since their property as felt rather than perceived, depends upon their being vague.

The complete aesthetic object which is a composed abstraction from things, with inner relations of direction and interval, is taken as a whole. If there is decomposition, it ceases to be a complex, and becomes at best a compound object. But if we avoid decomposition, it is one single thing with local differences, with felt inner distinctions. These distinctions are felt as belonging to the object, and as being inherent in the things that make up the object. That they do not really belong to the things inherently, is evident enough because of the way in which attention alters the relations. To how great an extent, however, the feelings are inner bodily feelings, is uncertain. Theorists who like simple and sweeping generalisations of their particular psychological fads, can answer the question offhand. Certainly there are many cases where the bodily feelings can be clearly detected, and their transference to the thing can be noted. In most cases this is not true, and the feelings may be qualities of vague ideas. For many psychologists such a statement has no meaning, but in any event, the answer is of no importance for aesthetics. One can stick to the fact, of a felt relation that makes the inventorial details ring in unison, and determines the aesthetic character of the object.

It can, and ought to, be objected, that there seems to be something theoretic in the denial that an aesthetic object is made up of perceived parts, for in a picture there are indubitably horses and cows, reds and blues, there are scenes and characters in plays, notes and phrases in music. That of course is true, but it is not these objects in describable relation that make up the aesthetic whole. They make the map, the decomposable whole. What makes the aesthetic whole is the way the edges grow together, as it were, the way one thing passes into another, the way the substance passes out of control of our measuring instruments, and in some indisputable way the local differences grow into one.

An analogy in the field of scientific interests is found in the notion of causality. Causality does not properly belong to science, because science is atomistic, and atoms could not conceivably get any closer to each other than to touch. But in order that there should be causality in any meaningful sense, something must go over from one thing to another. Causality seems to imply the contradiction of what is most fundamental for atomistic science—that two things cannot be at the same place at the same time. But that would seem to be necessary if one billiard ball is to be the cause of motion in another. If only there were a point where both were at the same time, there would be no difficulty whatever for one to carry on where the other left off, since they would be actually continuous. A monistic world would never have occasion to worry about this difficulty, since in a world which was already one, nothing could be so finally and definitely outside anything else as to make continuity impossible.

The aesthetic object is just such a world. The atomic spot of colour, line, word, sound, is local in space and time, but this is in no adequate sense an element of composition. The composition is continuous, and the elements are not arrested at the limits where physically evident contours are placed. As compositional elements of the aesthetic whole, they go on and interpenetrate all the rest. Everything is where it is and it is everywhere else as well. Clear localised perception and vaguely localised feeling, are inextricably confounded and commerced. One is all, and all is one. Here, there, now, then, everywhere and everywhen, all belong together, and nothing exists except as part of all the rest.

Though the world of aesthetics can never know the troublous problem of causality that comes from trying to establish a unity of things that are separate, it has the opposite trouble of finding separate things to unify. In a later chapter there is an attempt to show that causality is not a problem for knowledge at all, but in another sense we must pay attention to the relation of the parts of the whole. There is an aesthetic paradox that only through clarity and distinctness in the intervals, is a high degree of aesthetic expression possible. There must be no separation, and yet the separation must be distinct; there must be no parts, and yet the parts must be definite. This seems like a pretty mess of contradictions. The answer is to be found in the study of rhythm.

Life has been defined as "One darned thing after another," but one thing could not come after another, if something did not come to an end. We are hungry, we eat, and are no longer hungry. We are bored, and some good friend comes in to amuse us, and we are no longer bored. Something happens and runs its course, but while this course is running something else gets started, and then another thing. Life is a monstrous fugue, whose movement sinks and pauses at times in sleep or coma, but which ends in a full stop, perhaps, only when death ends all.

Action, except mere stretching and turning, or the idle threshing movements of a child, aims at an end. No living thing could look forward with equanimity to a movement that would go on forever. Our imagination soon demands a goal. Curiously enough, even to continue is to look forward to further goals. We are so made that out of every continuum we make a concatenation, we put in links where to the observer there would be continuous motion. When we rush along a road we note the things that mark our going, we pant to go faster, we want to go slower, we want to go elsewhere. We want change, but to change means to alter a goal. We want something else, always something more, or something other, or more of the same thing, which, every time that it is demanded, becomes in so far forth something else.

When we have reached a definite goal we do not want to stay forever. We are off again. And then once again. And then once more. And so on till the end.

In life as it is practical, the end is something to rest in. We want a meal because we are hungry, we want a fire because we are cold, we want company because we are lonely. When we get what we want we stop complaining for a while, or else we ask for something else. But when we dance we act otherwise. One step or group of steps brings us to a goal, but we go on and do it over again. We maintain an identical direction and the same goal recedes and again and again recedes. Only when the music stops does the series of steps end in the solution of repose. In a way this process is like life, but in a way it is different.

The difference that is here important is that in the dance the direction is determinate, and that endings and beginnings are related by the measure of their intervals. The scheme of life, in contrast, appears irrational. It contains currents that cannot be correlated with the rest, that render meaningless the purpose of life. A microbe, an earthquake, a broken promise, break up a given direction, and set up cross-currents that will not enter as a part of what has been foreseen.

Intermediate between the indetermination of life and the highly organised whole of a dance is such a thing as a dinner. This has a direction from soup to coffee and cigars, but there are no very definite relations of interval. We commonly eat less caviar or salted almonds than beef and potatoes, but the variations are indeterminate to a great extent. Bread and beverages are casually interspersed, in fact the rhythm of a dinner is far more explicit in the reading of a menu, than in the eating of it. The felt whole of a dinner is an almost perfect example of a low-grade aesthetic object.

The dance is as different from this as possible. To lose step is to end it lamely. One must begin again. Before the foot is put down in the last step of a single phrase, the terminal extension of the present into the future starts it off upon the next. When the music stops suddenly, the dancer is arrested as though in mid-air, even if his feet are both on the floor. He is genuinely in two places at once. His motions overlap, and are parallel, and continuous.

What is true of the dance is obviously true of music, and it is equally true of every other developed aesthetic object. No matter how simple this may be, so that it has position, direction, and intervals, it breaks into movements whose occasion is the summing of effects that extend backwards and forwards, looking beyond the immediate goal before that has been reached, to farther goals which take up the present ones into themselves, and keep the act going until a final resolution of the movement completes the whole in a comprehensive reverberation.

This is the reason why definiteness of intervals is perfectly consistent with the insufficiency for aesthetic uses, of fixed constituent elements. The elements which can descriptively be made clear and sharp, and which form a mosaic of the whole, are turned into an aesthetic continuum because we cannot stop to measure one before we leap upon the next. We must carry it along as best we can as we go hurtling through space, gathering up the parts that cannot make a sum but can only make a whole. While we are taking one in the actualising present, we are in an ideal present taking all the rest.

Tension is the concluding theme of this chapter. It is the quality of stress in a change of direction. There is an inertia in aesthetic experience as there is in mechanics, though the laws are different. The most conspicuous difference is that the laws are quite unknown, and possibly unknowable. Fatigue is involved and habituation. It may be easiest to move in straight lines or in circles. It is largely a matter of habit, though doubtless in part it depends on structure and muscular ease. A long straight line is difficult to maintain perfectly, unless it runs up and down, and a line of uniform curvature is easier than one which changes according to some regular system. But this sort of thing is not worth going into. The general conditions of tension are more important.

The crude expression of tension is obvious strain. Accent is obtained by stamping, shouting, pounding. Contrasts are of black and white, of colour complementaries, of up and down; and effects are obtained by conspicuous catastrophes, and obvious poetic justice. Refinement in tension leads to the substitution of delicate recovery for a nailed-to-the-mast symmetry; it flattens the obvious curve to a sensitive fluctuation; it makes possible the story with all the hazards of life retained, but so connected that coherence is itself a solution.

Tension is, I imagine, chiefly of two kinds—that of contrast, and that of continuity. An illustration of the contrast is Shakespeare's line,

In cradle of the rude imperious surge.

The number of marked contrasts is striking. Cradle-surge, rude-imperious, the contrast of vowels, and of the first and second half lines.

Compare with this, "When icicles hang by the wall," etc., where each line is like a loop in a lightly hung chain, or even like a cantilever easily in touch with its neighbour.

Tension in line can be observed if one will follow the outline of a vase and notice the force it requires to bend the line of the contour. This will depend upon the apparent elasticity of the line, the direction and energy imparted by the preceding portion, and so on. The subject is too large to be gone into here. It is necessary only to show the relation of tension to the other primary elements in aesthetic objects. Tension is the measure of vitality in intervals; intervals heighten the force of direction, and make it definitely expressive; and direction is the extension of place.

XIV. Pictorial Seeing

I F THE AESTHETIC OBJECT is a whole which gets its particular character from an object-maker who makes it because he has an interest in seeing things in relation to his self, then the way of seeing becomes a subject that must be studied as thoroughly as may be. It is the theme of the ensuing chapters.

My own particular interest in seeing became definite some twenty-five years ago. One day it occurred to me to ask, "What does a painter see when he paints?" Obviously the picture will not tell you how he sees the thing from which the picture derives, because the picture is a translation in terms of a particular medium, of the thing seen. Of course the experienced artist who has painted many pictures which are all more or less alike, will get the habit of seeing anything which he intends to paint, in terms of his pictures which are already familiar, but I was not concerned with the vision of a thoroughly conventionalised artist. What is it, I wanted to know, that the artist sees, who tries to see freshly. I concluded that the only way to know how others see was for oneself to learn to see, and I set to work at that. I put a plate on a table, and for six weeks I looked at that plate every day for some minutes or hours.

I had no definite plan when I began to look at the plate. My enquiry could best have been worded in conundrum form—How does a plate look when it is not a plate but a picture? There was no way to go about it except to continue looking with the question in one's mind, until the result came to pass. This happened at the end of about six weeks. The transformation has already been spoken of at length in terms of the distinction between the inventorial and the aesthetic object. Here it is important only to mark the point that what counts, is not the idea but the experience. It is important to see things, not to know that others see them. In a world where it is supposed that philosophy can be learned by reading without thinking, where art is supposed to be susceptible of "explanation," it is worth stressing this fact. There is no need of being serious about one's aesthetic experience, but if one is to be serious, the effort must be expended in seeing and not in reading. The only book of value is one that enables the student to dispense with it, that sends him off to use his eyes.

For a long time after my experience with the plate, I continued to do the same sort of thing with whatever came before my eyes. At one moment or another I would begin to look at things pictorially, until the capacity was greatly developed, and could make a picture of almost anything. Then it happened one day, as I was sitting in the dining-room of a remote little hotel in the French Alps, that I noticed a chromo advertisement of some liqueur. The picture showed a bottle, a glass, a coffee-pot, a cup, a sugar-bowl, a cigar, an ash-receiver. The artist had carefully arranged his material, and had drawn the things with skill. None the less the picture, though only a little one, was curiously sprawling in character. The reason was evident if one examined it carefully. One could then see that the artist when once he had arranged the elements with care, was content to draw them bit by bit. He looked at the cork when he drew the cork, then at the neck of the bottle and drew that, and so for all the rest. He knew that a picture must be composed, but he seems to have taken it for granted that an arrangement could be depended on for a pictorial composition. With each step in the painting he changed the focal centre of his vision, with the result of getting a group of well-drawn details, but which would make a picture only for one who was aesthetically as badly cultivated as himself. As a description of measurable and definable objects, his reproduction was better than a better picture would have been. It was not bad because it was full of realistic detail, but because the detail was separately seen. The competent work of art is a result of seeing all the things that enter into it, in a comprehensively centralised relation to the seer, and this is not the way that the maker of the lithograph saw them. What he got as a result was not so much a bad picture, as no picture at all. It would be more accurate to call it a group of painted objects.

The museums are full of pictures that fail, more or less, in the respect that the chromo failed in, completely. Some of these pictures have much merit of one kind or another, but our conventional habit of going to museums, and studying art in terms of so-called masterpieces, does comparatively little to lead to accurate discrimination in such fundamental characters. Pictures are such complicated things, that it is difficult to get a significant approach to them, and the tendency of criticism is to make schematic partitions that sound as though they ought to lead somewhere but actually do not. Consequently artists are generally contemptuous of lay critics and in general they are right. But the deficiency of the lay critic is far more the result of his deficient habits of seeing than of his want of practice as a painter. In many cases the critic does paint more or less, but this does not help him because he knows little or nothing of his own seeing habits. He is often a bad painter and does not see significantly, but even if he does both see and paint well, his lack of understanding of the process makes his criticism fragmentary and awkward. But as I said in my second chapter, criticism is altogether a rather unimportant matter. What is important is to have good seeing habits, which are developed along the lines on which aesthetic seeing is naturally laid. Seeing will then act naturally as a selective criticism, and verbal criticism can be confined to technical correction, and general conversation or its printed equivalent. Serious criticism applies to methods rather than to results, and if the method is right, that is, if the seeing is constructively right, then the thing seen will be exactly the measure of the seeing power so far developed.

There is then only one way to come to the understanding of the unity of aesthetic vision, and that is to get the habit of seeing that way. If one does this, if one learns to see with a controlled vision, one will soon get to understand how particular a competent painter's seeing is. Of course I do not mean it to be taken that the painter has thought specifically about the way he sees. Nor do we in the least know how he comes to see that way. We must assume a relatively high potential of energy, which helps him to his goal. This is why creative activity is so often accompanied by emotional disturbance, and why it often follows immediately upon a partial release which is analogous to a stage of psychoanalytic illumination. This is also a condition that makes for increasing unification, at least temporarily. The "natural" man probably has the same tendency to some degree, but apart from practical interests where the definite concentration is mostly on the production of instruments, he tends rather to a strung-along kind of existence. The creative person seems to be held up at the station beyond the next, and therefore to be maintained in a condition of suspense and crowding, awaiting a solution. Unification would come as the natural result of such anticipations stretching into progressively greater futures, as more and more of the past experiences are definitely related to a changing time foreseen. Education in seeing, like education in scientific discovery, is a deliberate cultivation of this mode of realising things.

To illustrate aesthetic seeing I shall take some of the ways in which I can see a brass candlestick on the mantelpiece before me. The ordinary way of seeing that candlestick would be to look it up and down, and to get an impression from it that does not exactly correspond to what the candlestick looks like at any single moment. When I do this I see the candlestick as the painter of the chromo saw the collection of things on his table. Suppose that I change my way of seeing, that I look at the base and without removing my attention from it as focal I take in the whole of the candlestick. Of course I must be at a sufficient distance from the mantelpiece to make this easy. I notice that now the candlestick is shorter than it seemed before, and thicker, at least relatively. If I slowly raise my eyes and pause at the top, and once more see the whole but with the focal attention at the top, the candlestick will have grown tall and slender. In the first case the contour lines had all swept downwards into the base, and in the second case they swept upwards to the top. In both these cases, the effective unity of impression is greater than when I looked up and down. Of course I can also look at the candlestick with the focal centre taken at any other point, and for purposes of composition some other point might be better. I took the top and bottom because so the contrast is the greatest, and the composition was most easily made.

In my chapter on Distortion (Chapter XII) I dealt with the fact that aesthetic seeing always distorted the things seen, because seeing things in felt relation meant a union in which no one of the things maintained its inviolability of shape. This is inevitable, because any seen object composed of elements is not their sum, but the result of the influence that they mutually exert on each other. Every difference, no matter how slight in the way of taking them, produces a different object. Therefore every aesthetic object is unique, unless it is an actual replica of another. The amount of difference may be negligible for one purpose, and important for another. But in any case it is true that aesthetic experience means discovery or rediscovery. Aesthetic perception is the endless creation of novelties, as long as the perception is a living process. Habituation does play an important part, but only as the aesthetic value of an environment. In that case our real interest is another, and the aesthetic characters serve as a sustaining medium.

A consequence of the unique character of the aesthetic object is the impossibility of analysis. We are often served with analyses of particular works of art, but these are insufferably crude. The real analysis does not go beyond the noting of a few characters that are equally the property of the most diverse objects. All the rest is mere description, which is intelligible in proportion that the reader is ignorant. This is true of unintelligible things generally. They are understood only in so far as the reader is incapable of discovering that he does not understand. The poor are envious of the rich, the lowly envy the high-placed, but the uncomprehending do not envy the intelligent. They understand so much more than the latter do, that they have everything to lose, and nothing to gain, by changing places. Anyone who tries to make distinctions clear can testify to the truth of this. But explanations that do not explain are always welcome.

Because aesthetic analysis is so nearly impossible, so nearly meaningless, aesthetic education can only take the form of practice. One can only be taught how one ought to look, what positions to take with reference to that which is to be seen aesthetically, and where the attention should be directed in order that what is looked at should be seen. In so far as the aesthetic object serves chiefly for comfort, there is, of course, an inclination toward the accustomed. "I love everything that's old,— old friends, old times, old manners, old books, old wine." The world of art becomes a reinforcement of the easy-chair. It is then essentially as important as the easy-chair. Of course this importance is great, but there is not much to be said about it. My next chapter deals at greater length with pictorial seeing, and the assumption that underlies it is an imputed importance for aesthetic experience, that will justify the effort which it demands if it is to be something more than a conventionally refined repose. Hobbes long ago said when someone expressed surprise at the smallness of his library, that he would know no more than other men did if he read as much as other men do. It is rare for a vital thinker to be a great scholar. It is so easy to read and so difficult to understand, that it can hardly be over-emphasised that learning is doing, seeing, thinking. This is more true in aesthetics than anywhere else, because the vocabulary of aesthetics is vague to the point almost of being without meaning, and only the practice of seeing can give it a content.

XV. To Make Pictures
by Seeing Them

IT IS SIMPLER FOR the further study of aesthetic perception, to rest within the limits of that which is perceived with the eyes. What is true of vision, is in some analogous way true elsewhere, but the visual field is the simplest to set forth, and is also the one that I know best. I shall therefore stay within it for the most part.

The visual space will be conceived as a cube, a three-dimensional space. It contains planes which cross the line of vision, and planes which are more or less parallel to the line of vision—those which give breadth and height, and those which give depth. They may cross at any angle, and they may run inwards or upwards, more or less directly. Typical planes are those of earth and sky, of the walls of houses, of the enclosing surfaces of bodies, or fruits, or utensils. Planes may be made of disparate things which become continuous for purposes of composition, as when we look down the perspective of a street and make continuous planes of houses on opposite sides of the street, or when a person on one side is balanced by a lamp-post on the other. The continuity of planes has nothing to do with the actual continuity of the things, any more than the continuity of a game of chess depends on someone moving a piece the moment the other man has moved his.

The possibilities of plane construction within a space are infinitely great, and we shall have to consider in this chapter, the ways in which controlled attention makes planes enter into combinations that are aesthetically valuable. I am not interested in the quantitative laws that have at times been worked out to determine the placing of the planes in certain mathematical order, and I have no opinion of their value. My own concern is with the characteristic qualities of the order. If there are really numerically determinable relations, they would be of a kind to satisfy conditions of the sort that I shall describe.

What, in general, is the satisfactory result that can be demanded of an arrangement of planes in space? The answer was given in what we said of rhythms. A complete picture is a space presentation, in which the space is so completely filled with the rhythmic resonances, that there is no room for anything else. A picture is something that one looks into, but that one keeps out of. If one feels impelled to walk down the pictured road, or climb the pictured mountain, or kiss the pictured girl, or eat the pictured peaches, the picture is, in so far forth, not a picture. It is a group of painted things, with which one enters into non-pictorial relations. What makes good pictorial advertisement makes a bad picture, and the good picture is not right for advertising purposes. The advertisement should make one want to be a partaker, while the picture leaves one content as a knower. The advertisement is completed by the inclusion of the possible customer, while the picture is completed by such a utilisation of the contained space, by such a reciprocating play of the intervals, that entrance could be made only by a rupture of the existing order. A picture is a rhythmically ordered spatial whole. *Picture* can stand figuratively for any aesthetic object whatever.

Rhythm is a movement that tends to come to rest, that is taken up and carried on despite partial assimilations, and which is concluded only when the vibrations are stilled by their diffusion through the whole. In such a case the composition is alive. The aesthetic object completely exists only so long as this cyclic movement can be produced, and only for him for whom it can be brought to pass. There are no objects that are aesthetically valid for all persons and at all times, but the nearest to an absolute aesthetic object is probably a simple symmetrical thing like a cross, which has elementary relations to a fundamental bilaterality. As soon as there is complication in the elements, there is uncertainty in the adjustment, and room for personal idiosyncrasy, and also for merely momentary responsiveness. What lasts for a lifetime without going dead for one person, lasts two minutes for another, or no time at all. The kind of standardised valuations that one finds in the textbooks and in popular lectures, need not correspond to any real responses of the writer. They are the expressions of a practicable average, and are only useful for conversation.

A permanently satisfactory aesthetic object, for a fully competent observer, cannot exist, because it is always an attempt to give in arrested form the quality of movement. In elementary symmetry the movement is at a minimum, and the success in expression is at a maximum. But with increasing richness of the movement, there is increase of fallibility. The movement can only be suggested, it cannot be rendered, and it tends to go dead when it is looked at too long. Therefore a work of art is like a sunset, in that the perfect moment for leaving it is when its splendour is at the fullest. Even as the colours of the sunset fade to ash, so the vitality of rhythms dies out in the perceived fixity of compositional elements, which can no longer be brought to vibrant coherency, but fall into a group of inventorial objects. Ichabod, Ichabod, the glory is departed! So has many a masterpiece gone its way to the ash-heap. Some have returned in answer to a resurrected sensibility, but many have remained on the ash-heap forever.

We must digress for a moment to point out in what sense it is true even for the arts of movement like poetry and music, that there is an attempt to express movement in static terms. The discrepancy in the movements there is the difference between the broader range of interest that is involved, and the narrower range of the actual expression.

Poetry is expression by symbols, not only by the mere symbols, where a word stands for a thing, but by symbols of a higher order where one thing stands for another. A poet who is in earnest, always means what he says, but he never says what he means. His meaning always goes far beyond his saying. He is giving a concrete and particular expression to a condition of things. Even if his intended meaning is for him bound up with that particular expression, that of his reader is not. What is implicated sweeps over, under, and round the objective statement. There are thousands of Shakespeares, and the Beethovens are almost as numerous. If this were not so, there would be more unanimity of opinion among readers. Some critics hold that it is the reader's duty to put himself in the author's place and to understand him, so far as possible, as he understood himself. Authors themselves, do not usually encourage this view, at least, they show a marked disinclination to explain themselves. Perhaps they are really wiser than the critics, and know more or less vaguely that if they have not expressed themselves in an unequivocal way, it is because they have not so understood the matter. In any case what they say is the ultimate public fact, to which the reader comes even as the author had come to his original material. The reader is under no other obligation to the author's possibly intended meaning, than the author was to nature's. For every succeeding stage, art and nature are as one. They are both public fact, to be used as occasion directs.

We return now to our specific theme, the rhythmic expression that shall have the quality of going on, of keeping the ball in play, of maintaining the aesthetic life. It is out of the question to establish any laws of rhythmic organisation—that would be far too pretentious. All that I can try to do is to point out what are the structural elements that make up the essentials of painting and sculpture, and afterwards to describe somewhat the attitudes that can make them effectual.

It must not, however, be supposed that aesthetic seeing is ever a facile thing. We are so accustomed to think of it as a form of relaxation, as a pastime, that the notion of it as an almost ascetic discipline is to most people incredible, or absurd. Why bother about it, except for fun? And it must be admitted that on the basis of current conceptions, there is no reason why one should. The real justification for my belief that there is a good reason must be left to the concluding chapters. Here it is sufficient to point out that pure aesthetic experience, that which takes the object objectively, requires the same singleness in one's motives as pure science does. The objects are different, but the integrity of objective reference is the same. This integrity means the holding together of the object without any intrusion of one's own irrelevant interests. Mozart said in an oft-quoted passage, that the great moment in composition was when the whole piece was present to him at an instant. The same is true for the real apprehension of any work of art. That maximal moment is the moment of completest dedication to the thing itself, and is the goal of aesthetic activity.

Aesthetic objects, it will be recalled, have the characters of place, direction and interval. In all those of a high order, directions are broken into series of intervals. These are, in the plastic and graphic arts, marked as planes. *Planes* is a somewhat conventional term for elements of any kind. Planes are intermediate between lines and volumes. Lines are reduced planes, and volumes are massive planes; therefore the word is the most suitable one for a generalised expression. When we speak of planes in what follows, we will mean compositional elements of any kind, in so far as they are held together as related intervals.

In a picture that is flat, these relations constitute a pattern which, when simple, is symmetrical with respect to one or more axes, and when more highly developed, is asymmetrical in any one of numberless ways. In recent years, especially because of Japanese influences, our sensibility to asymmetrical balance has greatly improved. The latest movements in art have pressed this still further, so that now, rhythms that are independent of any bilaterality, are familiar to all. It will therefore be easy for anyone to apply what I have said of rhythmic completeness to flat patterns, and so to lay a foundation for the understanding of the more complex structures of paintings which have depth, and of sculpture. These are more difficult to understand in principle, but they are, proportionately, still more difficult to see at all definitely. Success in flat composition is quite common, but complete success in three-dimensional composition hardly exists. The problem of the adequate handling of depth has been crucial for European art since the Middle Ages, and has been the cause of its comparative failure. It still remains the great difficulty, and the efforts to solve it in recent painting have not been at all satisfactory. It is worthwhile, therefore, to study it thoroughly.

Objects as they are represented on the planes that extend inwards into the picture diminish in size relatively to their distance, and they also undergo foreshortening. Since the ideal purpose, the perfect accomplishment in the three-dimensional composition is to fill the space through the completed rhythm of the things that enter into it, there is an obvious increase in difficulty when the measures in one direction are decidedly different from those in the other directions. Up and down, right and left, the rhythmic expression is easily made consistent, but the third dimension involves a different scale system, and greater difficulties.

There are obviously two ways in which planes can represent distance—they may be diagonal planes like perspective planes of houses or railroad tracks, or they may be transverse planes like the successive layers of scenery on the stage. In their eventual meaning they come to the same thing, because the successive planes are combined in our seeing to give continuities of diagonal planes, but it is well to keep the distinction in mind, since it will be seen in the outcome that it is the combination of the characters suggested by the two methods, which will give a satisfactory solution.

The diagonal planes find their most obvious use in presenting the depth of objects. People who have little sense of what a picture distinctively is, prefer landscapes which carry the attention inward toward a far horizon, and which even suggest spaces beyond that. They feel a profundity corresponding to the remoteness. But when this happens, the unity of the picture is lost. In looking at things in this way, one is more like a person travelling through the picture than like one who is seeing it. To be sure the trip is taken only in imagination, but this is a minor distinction. A picture, I repeat, is something that we look into but keep out of, and in a later chapter I shall try to show that the difference between getting into and keeping out of the picture is a general difference between pure and applied aesthetics. If our contact with art really has an effect that amounts to much, the nature of the contact becomes important. This is not, at present, commonly the case, but even if the making of pictures were a mere trick, and the appreciation of pictures were nothing more than the appreciation of a trick well performed, it would be none the less true that a successfully made picture would have the qualities that I am now talking about. The whole of its actual or implied space would be filled with forms that organise in terms of rhythmic continuity, and in order that this completeness should be appreciated, the spectator would have to realise the significance of organisation in the perspective lines. The failure to handle depth rhythmically is the prevalent failure in Western art. It is only if we look at the problem as a distinct and particular one, that we can avoid the futilities of cubism on the one hand, and the failure of most treatments of depth, to keep the spectator out.

Almost everyone is now familiar with the practice of the Japanese who raised the farther ends of their perspective planes and made them look almost like diagonals that run across the paper. The Japanese may have learned this through their custom of drawing on the horizontal plane of the floor. If then the picture is hung on the wall, this characteristic effect will become evident. But however it may have come to pass, the value of this mode is that it makes a compromise between planes that break the continuity of the two-dimensional space by running inward, and planes that converse it by running across.

The value of this scheme has been widely recognised in European art even though it has not been used with the same frankness. Many artists tend to raise their horizons above the correct perspective level. Today this is done boldly as a result of Japanese influence, but it was done more or less independently before. Poussin, a French painter who worked in Rome during the seventeenth century, and who is perhaps the greatest master of landscape composition that has worked in the West, habitually used a high horizon, and Delacroix, in the early nineteenth century, repainted the landscape in an important picture after seeing a Constable with a high horizon.

The practical advantage of composing on a plane that slopes upward is obvious. The whole remains in view as one works upon it. Objects placed upon it are more completely seen, and there is less dependence upon aerial perspective, or upon the relations of diminishing size. In some oriental work these are almost wholly disregarded, but there is nothing in the nature of a sloping plane that is inconsistent with their use.

It is, however, not at all necessary that planes which run inward should have their perspective character distorted. They may be naturalistically drawn, and yet be so broken up with transverse planes as to become, not mere directions, but also compositions of intervals. A road that one is looking down, may have the trees that border it so treated, that instead of seeming to be no more than a road that agreeably leads into the distance, it becomes a rhythm of spaces that prevents the eye from finishing at the farther end. The interplay of rhythmic relations throws back to preceding portions, and keeps active the value of the whole. Mere direction is essentially mere continuity. One may, it is true, go down the line in either direction, but in only one at a time. With intervals that are rhythmically related, there are continually successive throwbacks, that keep up the movement in both directions. The characteristic defect in the treatment of depth is the neglect of this. The difficulties that are the results of the alteration in size, and of the foreshortening, are the causes of this in part, and in part the defect is due to lack of clear understanding, of the compositional relation of depth to the flat plane of the picture's surface.

When I go into a picture gallery I usually find that most of the canvases are not pictures at all in my sense of the word. At best, they are rarely complete pictures. The surface is often quite adequately treated but the third-dimensional space is usually either a mere direction, or else its intervals are incoherent. The cubists tried to avoid this difficulty by making this dimension exceedingly shallow. It is a curious contradiction that the cubists are the painters who try to eliminate the cube of space. They never make mere surface decoration, but on the other hand they almost never control effectively the relations in depth. These are shallow, vague, and insecure.

If the depth of pictures were always filled by obvious planes like roads, houses, meadows and hills, which could be intersected by equally obvious trees, cows, persons, the matter would be relatively simple, at least to the understanding, but the planes are often curves, like those which make up the roundness of fruit and flowers, of nudes and heads.

For this kind of thing description is of little value. Analysis is impossible except in a schematic way. There is only one way to sharpen one's perception. The education of the eye in practice is the only road to the comprehension of all this.

The first thing to understand is the *plane of a picture*. Suppose you are in a room which has a door opening into another room, preferably a small room, or a hall. If you stand in the first room looking toward the door, you can get one or other of two effects. If you make the plane of the door your focal plane, your plane of reference, you will see the room beyond, or the hall, very much flattened. It will look like a space, and even suggest a space of the actual size, but it will not be hollow or deep. If, then, you change your focal level to the further wall, you will notice that the space grows hollow and deep. The appearance of the further room has been completely altered by the change from the focal plane of its near, to the focal plane of its far, side.

Another experiment will make this clearer. When you are sitting opposite a person in a car, or opposite one who has his back against a wall, look at him while making a definite attempt to refer the thing seen to a plane that runs across the front of his face. Afterwards, change the plane of reference to the surface of the wall. A little practice makes this quite easy. One does this, not by straining the eyes to keep them fixed, but by directing the attention so that the eye repeatedly comes back to the chosen plane, and therefore tends to neglect what is otherwise seen. You will notice that when the focal plane is in front, the person looks like a picture, and when the focal plane is behind, the person looks like a statue. The essential difference between painting and sculpture is precisely this difference in the placing of the focal plane. The front plane is the plane of the frame, on which a picture is actually painted, while the rear plane is the plane of the background against which sculptured reliefs are seen. In ordinary practical looking we hold neither to one plane nor another but move about in a disordered way, and that is what most people want to do when they look at pictures or sculpture.

The popular idea of the frame is of a window through which one sees into the picture. The righter idea is that the frame establishes a plane, to which the other planes indicated in the picture are referred. This makes clear the importance of the transverse planes that mark the intervals on the lines running into the picture. A picture could, in fact, be conceived as made up only of transverse planes like successive layers of theatre scenery, in which the object would be to emphasise the intervals, rather than, as in naturalistic stage scenery, to blend and so obscure them. These transverse planes are the means for creating a series of intervals and therefore for producing rhythmic movement in the deep dimension of the picture.

Making pictures is not quite as simple as this analysis of planes might cause it to seem. In actual practice there is no clear separation of the composition in depth from the composition in breadth. The same elements serve for both, and the composition in breadth is so much easier than the other, that it usually carries off most of the effective attention. Deep space is given over to realisms of one kind or another, and to sentimentalities of distance. Therefore complete pictures are exceedingly rare. Deliberate analytic looking in which the rhythmic treatment of depth is selected for attention, is the most practicable way of coming to an understanding of this characteristic element of painting as it prevails in the western world.

A word more must be given to sculpture. Everybody has been hearing much of late about negro sculpture. It has even been acclaimed as the only real sculpture known. That of the Greeks, we are told, especially of the Greeks of the classical period, is not truly sculpture in the round, but only a collection of reliefs developed on the four sides of the body. There is some truth in this. If one looks at Greek or Egyptian sculpture, the flatness of the surfaces will be evident. Negro sculpture is very different from this. Here the body is round like a column, and a head is made like an egg. The consequences of this difference will be obvious if one bears in mind what I have said about planes of pictures and planes of sculpture.

When the eye encounters a polished cylinder, it is free to go to the end. Nothing stops it before it has reached the widest part. The nearer portion therefore bulges conspicuously. If it is shiny and catches the light, it bulges still more conspicuously. In this respect the sculpture of Brancusi, a polished copper boiler, and negro sculpture are alike. The focal plane is the plane of the widest part, and this widest part is far back. In Greek work, on the contrary, the naturalistic treatment of the figure preserves the characteristic flatness of the body, which is more pronounced in the male figure than in the female. Therefore each side presents the widest part as almost a surface character, and so the details of modelling upon it act rather like a relief.

The perpendicularity of planes to the line of vision is the most important of all facts for the understanding of art form. It is important and it is not obvious. Otherwise there would not be so much bad painting and sculpture in the world. The departure from design on a flat surface, leads to all these difficulties of design in depth, which the modern artists have tried to solve. Their solutions have been for the most part such poverty-stricken inventions as might be expected from artists who try deliberately to think out their problems. Their abstractions from natural things have been thin and uninteresting, because they saw no way of controlling richer and more naturalistic forms. The specific talent of the artist apart from his manual ability, is for seeing. When he virtually renounces this talent and depends for his result on speculative manufacture, he cannot give anything of great importance. Nature is infinitely richer in plastic suggestiveness than the imagination of any artist who renounces her manifold gifts. A rhythmic utilisation of that which is everywhere to be seen in breadth and depth, is the true road for painting and sculpture to take. It is the source of almost all the art that has hitherto been produced, which is intended to hold the interest as in itself sufficient. There are many objects of use which are beautiful, from Egyptian jars and Chou bronzes to the wall papers and textiles designed under cubist influences. But these are at their best as a part of a human environment. It is characteristic of the conventional museum-visiting, antiquity-collecting, spirit of recent times, that the distinction between these two kinds of things is lost. Though not, of course, an absolute distinction, it is an important one. The return to nature after the sterilising of art in the last few years, will bring it once again into its place.

It may seem to some readers of this book that more ought to be said about specific works of art, that Giotto and Piero della Francesca and Greco and Rembrandt and Cézanne and Renoir ought to be referred to, and "criticised." There is nothing of that sort here because it seems to me unprofitable stuff. Criticism as a process in which *I* tell you what I think, will do very little to teach you to see. Since there is, in my opinion, no importance in being able to distinguish good art from bad, though it may become important that one should live so as to find good art more to one's purposes than bad, the only thing that I can regard as valuable *and practicable*, is to show that certain ways of seeing will lead to a choice of better things. Any one that learns to see a figure as a whole in terms of rhythm, at the same time letting the eye find its mainstay back as far as it will go, will without any instruction soon learn the difference between Michelangelo or Della Quercia, and Rodin. If he doesn't, then Rodin will answer his purposes just as well, and perhaps better. Anyone who was relying upon the very best criticism a few years ago would have made great effort to see Rodin as the peer of Michelangelo, and as more than the peer of anyone else. The best criticism today regards this sort of thing as ridiculous. If it is ridiculous now, it was ridiculous then as some of us then thought it. On the other hand, it is never ridiculous to see as best one can with the means that one has. To improve one's means is to enrich one's world. Eldorado is Eldorado only for him that can enter thereinto.

XVI. Composition

IN THE CHAPTER ON Pictorial Seeing (Chapter XIV), I described some different ways in which a candlestick could be seen when one took it as a whole, but with different levels of focal reference. These different ways of taking it make different compositions. In this chapter the subject of composition will be given more extended treatment.

Let a person who is interested in understanding composition, stand back a little from a window and look out. Using the window frame as a picture frame, let him attend to the picture that appears within it. Let him move a bit to one side or the other, shifting his position till the view gets itself organised as satisfactorily as possible. If one can learn to do this and is really interested in pictures, he need never be bored as long as there is anything to look at which offers sufficient variety for compositional exercise.

One who does this will find the most remarkable alterations in things as they take their place in different compositions, for, of course, there is no *one* composition to be seen in a particular frame. It will commonly happen when no particular effort is made, that some dominant elements will determine some picture as the most obvious one to be seen, but a change of interest will alter the proportionate importance, and consequently change everything.

A good picture has characteristically a centre of focal reference about which the elements balance. There may be something represented at this centre, or it may be an empty space. In any event it need not be, and generally is not, a point to which we pay special attention, any more than that we pay attention to the centre of the circle in looking at a circular design. It is rather a point, or a region, which is implied by the relations of the elements in the picture, a kind of centre of gravity. The choice of some controlling features in the making of the picture, will establish the position of this centre, and the rest of the compositional members will be selected and placed to confirm and enrich the indicated rhythm.

The choice of these elements is, of course, not made explicitly and with deliberate intention. It is rather the result of a natural selection which becomes more subtle and precise as the seeing-in-compositional-terms habit grows. Things are included or left out as the composition forms itself, without one's being at all aware of what one is including or leaving out. For instance, I have a view from where I am writing, of which I am fond. There is a broad avenue, a railroad embankment with a roundhouse and shops at one end, and in the distance, a line of houses ending with the dome and tower of a church. I have fallen into the habit of taking this view in a certain way, and once it occurred to me to ask what details I included and what I left out. I was surprised to see how many conspicuous objects I habitually did not see when I was looking pictorially. Of course when I am doing it on purpose, and want a change, these other factors may be made to enter. I wish merely to point out that the picture-making faculty is positively selective.

Composition in depth is as important for pictorial seeing as it is for painting. Just as in painting, it is the more difficult thing, and is that which makes the seeing rigorous and unsentimental. It is almost unbelievable how much sheer plastic beauty can be wrought out of a commonplace street scene by the creation and co-ordination of imaginary planes thrown across the street from house to house, with lines of roofs, cornices, or other saliences serving as means of attachment. Hill country becomes transformed when the lines are made to serve in a definite way instead of rolling accidentally. By moving the pictorial planes backward or forward, masses are flattened or developed at will. The plasticity of natural materials is in fact almost infinite, if only one has learned to mould them.

I began by instancing the use of a window as a frame, but this is only a convenience for beginners. With a little practice, one can virtually have a frame wherever one wants one. One can make pictures wherever one looks, by merely flattening the planes. One's desk with multifarious objects becomes a still life; a café, a restaurant, or a drawing-room, becomes a pictorial interior; pictures happen everywhere that one is minded to look for them. Although I have always been more interested in painting than in any other art form, yet I consider the capacity to see pictorially as more important than the seeing of pictures. It goes without saying that one's capacity to see pictorially has been nourished by one's experience of pictures, but it is something very different from the tendency to see nature in terms of the latest painter in whom one has become interested. It is a positive exercise of faculty, and one which is richly creative.

It is for this reason that this kind of pictorial seeing is as far as possible from day-dreaming. It is, in fact, an effective way of preventing this and of substituting for the mooning kind of landscape apprehension which is so common, a robust perception that is a genuinely creative visual activity.

Another interesting practice in composition is to change the general character of the picture according to the medium that one prefers to use. Everybody knows that pictures can be made in line or in masses, in black and white or in colour, but few people know that one can also see in terms of these different mediums. It is, however, entirely possible. The capacity of selective interest to alter the nature of what one is looking at is surprisingly great, and the transformations that one can effect, for instance by bringing out the colour from an apparently drab crowd of people, merely by intending to see it in terms of colour, seems almost miraculous.

It is one of the conventional deliverances whenever art is spoken of, that art differs from nature because in art there is selection while in nature there is none. Perhaps there is none in nature, but in seeing nature there is a great deal. But when people say selection, they usually mean arrangement. We saw in a previous chapter that well-arranged objects are perfectly compatible with seeing that is aesthetically of a very low grade. This statement about selection would have more meaning if the mind were, as was formerly believed, essentially a blank sheet on which nature printed itself. Since this is not at all the case, since all seeing is selection, more can be done by educating this selective faculty than anyone would suppose who has not tried it. Selection is inevitable, therefore it may as well be directed to some desirable end.

In respect to composition, as elsewhere in matters of art, the most useful kind of criticism is the implicit kind that comes from one's own developed habits of seeing, which makes one critically selective when looking at the things that artists make. Almost nothing can be said about their composition except that it does or does not achieve the kind of thing that I have been speaking of, unless one is competent to go further and to say, in precise detail, what is the matter, to point out what changes should be made to bring about the desired result. The lay critic almost never pretends to this competence, and usually offers some description of the picture which is nothing more than a crude translation into words of what can be far more precisely seen. That sort of thing has value only for the most elementary purposes of calling the spectator's attention to that which is rather obvious.

It is only in a generalised form that this is at all useful, but it can never be effective for describing particular works of art. The particular work is always dependent for its individual value upon adjustments of intangible minuteness, so that description is impossible. This is well illustrated by the fact that damaged originals are often better than well-preserved copies, made when the picture was in better condition. The copy may give information about the original, but it rarely satisfies us. None the less, no description can ever come as close to the original as such a copy does. Verbal analysis, and verbiage about particular pictures, are useless. Analysis cannot go beyond general characters, and must leave the specific ones to be seen in the work itself.

XVII. Some Aesthetic Fields Unrecognised

THE CONVENTIONAL LIMITATION OF the interest of aesthetics to art and to beauty in nature, has helped to make the subject unintelligible. I have taken pure aesthetics to be a cognitive attitude in which things are known through the co-ordinate of the self, that is, through feeling. In this chapter I wish to bring to attention some important fields of interest where objects are constituted in that way, and which therefore belong to aesthetics. Their neglect has wronged many a poor man who has been turned away from the only region of aesthetic interest open to him, and who has been led "to fool with pictures and fans," as though aesthetic salvation could only be found there.

A stamp collector is not usually thought of as concerned with aesthetics, but what is it that makes such a collector interested in the completeness of his series, and the condition of his particular examples? Of course it might be only the spirit of competition, to do something difficult and beat other people. This would, however, not explain the particular form that it takes. The same thing might be true of an architect who might want to build a bigger cathedral or a more beautiful cathedral than someone else had built. But if this were the real motive the one would not be very much interested in his collection, nor the other in his cathedral. In fact, the collection becomes, in the terms that we have worked out in a previous chapter, a concrete symbol for one of the predominant self-feelings, that of completeness, of finality. Essentially the same kind of an interest that will make one person construct an ideal system in which everything is accounted for, from the atom to God, will make another try to get every stamp that ever was printed, and to have them all as perfect as possible. What to the one is given by the ideal harmony of the cosmic system, is given to the other by perfectly filled sheets.

It is very common for neurotics to be annoyed by incompleteness, and irritated by the indifference which practical men show in the matter of equipment. Their ideal completeness often far outruns any accomplishment to come, and their magnificently prepared programme is often their total result. In this case, as in many others, the neurotic serves as an exaggerated specimen of the character which in its moderate quantity forms a desirable component of a balanced character. Making collections may depend upon an acquisitive impulse, but the interest in the quality of the collection depends upon something else, and making this interest effective, is essentially an aesthetic activity.

The same thing is true of the book collector. He may be sad when he thinks of some imperfection in a rare book, though he may not have looked at the book for ten years. The adjustments that he makes are very curious. He may be rejoiced to have a copy of an absolutely rare book in very bad condition, while a book just a bit less rare, in that condition, would disgust him. I have an old Italian table of which the top has been hacked and gashed and burnt and hammered, but there was a time, when if I found on it the least little new scratch, I was upset. One's idealities can find the most absurd conciliations, but on the given level they are often adamantine in their claims.

Surgeons often speak of a beautiful operation, and engineers of a beautiful job, and if beautiful and aesthetic worth are to be taken as equivalent, their use of the term is accurate. The surgeon does not mean that the sight is beautiful, but he does mean that the operation is typical, a perfect expression of a felt interest, and therefore he is right to call it beautiful. Civilisation loses a great deal through the failure to perceive, and to avail itself of the consequences of aesthetic values, in practical affairs. This is especially marked in the case of the businessman.

There seems to be growing in America today a new businessman's religion, the religion of service. It differs from most of the religions of more or less civilised peoples in the past, by skipping the initial period of other-worldliness. It starts as a businessman's religion, instead of being made one when it has become a social success. Up to a recent time the businessman accepted the onus of being in business to make money. He got his religion outside, and his aesthetic satisfaction also. Often he retired more or less from affairs and tried to get both culture and pleasure from travel, from visiting art galleries, and reading books. Of course, the attempt was rarely successful. Such an exclusive devotion to art is abnormal except for the artist. People who try that sort of thing do not realise that effective aesthetic experience implies effective aesthetic interest, and that the proper place to get it is where one's interest lies. I do not know how much of aesthetic interest there is combined with the new businessman's religion, but certainly an interest of that kind which was aesthetically genuine, and not sentimental, could have far-reaching consequences.

Pure aesthetic interest, like pure scientific interest, is committed to an attitude of mental honesty. The feelings implicated must be authentically expressed in the picture, and cannot accept a substitute. If it were recognised that vital aesthetic interest has no particular connection with "art" but is solely concerned, in Matthew Arnold's phrase, "To see things steadily, and see them whole," then it would be obvious that the civilised man of affairs would find the necessity of seeing his activities *in general* in that light. It would be a defect in business or in politics that one would have to do things which one looks at askant, a practically far more serious defect than any lack of sincerity in the painter or poet. The really underlying questions that are concerned here, have to do with the coherence of personality which will be touched on in the chapter on Selves (Chapter XX). Here I must be satisfied to point out that aesthetic interest can be vital only where interest is genuine; that the scientist will find it chiefly in science, the explorer in exploring, the politician in politics, the businessman in business. But this always implies the condition that one's interest in these things extends beyond mere exploitation. The temper of mere exploitation is never the temper of knowing, and therefore is not the temper of science or aesthetics. I began the paragraph about the aesthetics of business by speaking of the businessman's religion, precisely because that attitude implies an interest beyond exploitation. If it were made a thing genuine and sincere and unafraid to look all facts in the face, there is no reason why it should not become as full and desirable a world of beliefs as any other. Its plastic material is the richest conceivable—men's bodies and souls, their human and social welfare. Unless pictures and fans and Wayside Inns are made subsidiaries in the whole picture of Man in Industry, the aesthetic result will not amount to much.

If the *beautiful* meant the pretty, current attitudes toward the aesthetic would be more justifiable. But to Beauty is attributed a lofty dignity of character that is almost incompatible with a picture gallery, and the spirit that goes with it. Plato's *Republic* has more of the temper of serious aesthetic criticism than most of what deliberately intends to be such. As long as things that are nice to look at, or to listen to, are considered the real subject matter of aesthetics, for so long the artist will remain what society has made him—something between a household pet and a public nuisance. Only the recognition of the fact that all things have their aesthetic aspects, and that it is essentially uncivilised to ignore these, can correct this absurdity. When that change in view takes place we shall no longer see men of putative sense and dignity scrambling in the auction rooms for trivial rarities, while most of the significant aesthetic opportunities in the world go unregarded.

XVIII. Pure and Applied Aesthetics

I HAVE BEEN INTERESTED IN aesthetics since boyhood, and many times in the last twenty years I have thought to write a book on it. Every now and then I would come upon an idea that seemed both valid and important, and the book would get under way, but soon the idea would turn out either invalid or unimportant. Even if it was not quite so bad as this, it would prove insufficient to carry much of a load, and the book would end prematurely. Many books were written by others on aesthetics, and some of these I read. None of them seemed to go very far toward lighting up the paths along which I wanted to travel. Benedetto Croce of Naples, and the Freudians, wrote the most influential of recent books, and a German psychologist, Theodor Lipps, wrote the most influential book before their vogue began. I shall try to tell in a few words what each had to say.

Lipps taught that the qualities of form were a transference to the object of feelings, interests, impulses in the observer, which he had studied especially with references to felt poises and directions. Lines, surfaces, masses, get their specific quality of life from the life of the beholder, which is projected into them, for in themselves they have neither direction nor rhythm. Lipps did not relate these feelings of the objects to present or accompanying bodily reactions. He concerned himself with the fact that these things are in the mind irrespective of their origin, and it is the felt movement that is transferred, and not some particular present muscular activity.

The teaching of Lipps has to some extent become the commonplace of more recent psychological aesthetics. But as so often happens with psychology when applied to other matters, nothing comes of it once the stage of the general idea has been passed, except vagueness and diversity of opinion. It is only when statistical methods are applicable that progress is at all steady, and statistical methods in aesthetics have given only the most trivial results. Intelligence tests can be referred to for a contrast. There are endless disputes concerning that which is measured by these tests, and if the subject could not be advanced except by analysing intelligence, the subject would be of interest only to psychological investigators. Statistical methods have made of the testing something that concerns the world in general. Psychological aesthetics, having no statistics of importance, could not go beyond analysis. Only the Freudian studies of the relation to art of repression, compensation, and sublimation, have applied psychological analysis to aesthetics with enough success to reach and influence the public.

There are two sides to Freud's teaching in this matter, which have very different authority. Freud was the first person who systematically worked up the relation of sex conditions to the artist and art activities. Much of the material was, of course, well known, but Freud gave it a more comprehensive setting and a much more thorough treatment. No one who is familiar with the literature can question the value of his initiative in the recasting of artistic biography, and the social history of art.

For the other side of the subject of aesthetics, however, the side of formal art, of the interest in aesthetic perception in general, Freud's contribution is far more questionable. Here he has done nothing more than to make an application of his general scheme of the way that arrested sex impulse finds other outlets. He is in line with the current tendency of psychology to make organic impulse basic, and he has given to this kind of explanation, a peculiar limitation. He believes in a sexual instinct which is never very clearly defined, and which is the determinant for most of the developments in the mental life of man.

I have never been able to take much interest in this doctrine nor in the hostility which has often been shown it, because I cannot in the least understand it. Freud somewhere says that specific sexual causation is chemical, presumably glandular secretion, but he does not pretend to show that, in fact, any particular chemical conditions are present in the cases of what he calls sexual function. He has all sorts of ways of finding out whether or not sexual influences are present in one instance or another, till the reader gets to have a suspicion that there is a special Freudian divining-rod for this kind of thing. There is not the slightest evidence that Freud's *libido* is anything in particular, and therefore it was inevitable that Jung should have been driven to make *libido* mean vital energy in general. This way of regarding it adds nothing of explanatory nature, but neither does it take anything away. It breaks down the nominally clear distinction between sexual and ego instincts, but since the clarity never went far beyond the obvious fact that the two words are spelt differently and have a different moral and social flavour, there was no great loss in this. Freud's derivation of aesthetic interest from sex is entirely speculative, and has not illuminated the subject in the least.

Another defect of Freud's method that shows itself here as elsewhere, is his passion for deriving everything from something else that is remotely, or preferably, nearly like it. Because one ate sausages with peculiar avidity in early infancy, one retains a passion for sausage-like form in art forever after. Of course no evidence is offered for this except the persistence of neurotic traits. But this, of course, proves nothing more than that *if* the traits are neurotic, then this sort of persistence is probable. In the neurosis there is a line of arrested development. These arrests in development and the consequences of them, were Freud's particular theme. He has carried them over into other fields as though they were a sufficient basis for analogies everywhere. The crucial question of the legitimacy of the proceeding is never discussed.

We know exceedingly little of normal development in man, by which I mean development uninfluenced by regressive conditions. The normal man is not one who has grown up without being influenced by his education, for a man could not grow up that way at all, but he is one who assimilates that education to the conditions presented by his genuinely *contemporary* environment. He lives in the present, in contact with really current conditions, and has no psychic barriers that hold him back, in spots, to conditions that ought to have been outlived. Probably no man is completely free of these, which makes for the great difficulty of studies of development. Freud, whose interest is in these hold-backs, makes them the starting point for everything else, a certainly illegitimate proceeding. J. B. Watson began the study, with infants, of a real natural history of the mental life, although he declines to call it that. He found out something exact about the native reactions of babies. If that sort of thing could be carried on to puberty, under test conditions, so that regression could be avoided, we would reliably know something of the matter that the Freudians treat so arbitrarily. We should find out what are the emergencies of fresh qualities and aptitudes, and how far they are conditioned by the past, by education. At present the subject is in a haze. The psychoanalysts have been able to produce a certain effect because the facts of regression, and their consequences, are indubitable. As explanations of aesthetic interest in general, their theories are mere speculations, and are valuable only as occasions for further research.

The influence of Croce has been very different from that of Freud. Freud complicated the subject of aesthetics in a way that fascinated many persons, and repelled many others, as is inevitable when the aberrations of sex are put at the focal centre. Croce simplified the subject of aesthetics by proving to the satisfaction of many, especially men of letters, that the whole thing could be put into six sentences, or less if they were long ones. His account is not a psychological one, but is referrable to his theory of knowledge. Like most things of that kind it has a certain meaning for technicians in the subject, who know what are the questions that one ought not to ask. It is almost impossible to make clear a theory like Croce's to the layman, but since it has been quite popular of late, I shall try.

Croce is an idealist, that is to say, he believes that existence is fundamentally mental. This mental universe is somehow, in itself, without form and void. The process by which it takes form is analogous to the fiat by which, in Genesis, the world was created. The difference is that in Croce's process the creator is immanent in the world, and his creative operation was not ended in six days but is continuous. The transformation, which is a knowing process, is a forming of the mental chaos into objects of two kinds, which are known as aesthetic and logical. The former class of objects is made up of individuals, of particulars, which have *character*. The other class is made up of general ideas, of concepts, which can be united in propositions, and which are *true or false*. To note anything, is to subject the mental chaos to the formative influence of the creative fiat in an initial expression, that is, to characterise it, and thereby to give it aesthetic existence. Therefore, any contact with anything that gives it existence as a mental fact—there is no other kind—is an expression of the thing through the creative will which is itself mind. It is in this way that Croce identifies mental fact in its first emergence from chaos, as aesthetic; and, for him, art is nothing more than a complicated form of such a mental fact. Art is mind as characterising, and as character. The work-of-art is the materialised embodiment of that which is already art when it is conceived in the mind. A complete imaginative conception is already a complete aesthetic and artistic expression, though in practice it generally requires an embodiment in material form to enable the artist to work out his idea.

The whole of Croce's positive contribution to aesthetics is set forth in the preceding paragraph. His book on the subject is a large one, but most of the space is taken up with criticisms of the views that he does not agree with. The popularity of his work has not depended at all upon his philosophical basis, for his admirers are not for the most part interested in the theory of knowledge. What takes them is his essential brevity, for though this quality is not present in his writing, it is in his ideas. Croce places his proof in a region whither his disciples do not follow him, and when he comes down from the clouds with the simple assertion that it is all as easy as two-and-two-make-four, they take his word for it. The principal service of Croce to aesthetics has been to almost wipe out the subject, while leaving the word. This service is considerable, because aesthetics has been on the whole so enticing and so unprofitable, that its removal from the field of practical attention was a real boon.

I have not a very high opinion of Croce's aesthetics. I agree with him that knowledge is twofold, but I think that this can be shown in the actual conditions of knowing, and without any recourse to the hocus-pocus of the theory of knowledge. Furthermore by keeping the whole subject on the level of ordinary things, it can be made to contribute something more that a few abstract propositions. It can be made serviceable for the extension of one's actual aesthetic grasp.

The work of Lipps and Freud is far more valuable, but it has the defect, for the person who is interested in aesthetics without being a psychologist, that its development at once leads into fields of research where everything is obscure. This is not true of Freud's contribution to biography, but of his contribution to aesthetic fundamentals.

It is rather a curious thing how forgetful men of science are. It would seem that a scientist who had undertaken to supply a theory of art would feel the need for accounting for *any* work of art. Whitehead, in his *Introduction to Mathematics*, says that "Mathematics as a science commenced when first someone, probably a Greek, proved propositions about *any* things or about *some* things, without specification of definite particular things." So in general when one asserts propositions about any *kind* of thing. I was always discouraged in reading about theories of art and aesthetics, by the instances that I could think of which the writers were neglecting. My own practice of aesthetic vision had convinced me that the field was almost if not quite as broad as

Croce claimed it to be, but it seemed to me to have far more definite properties than he ascribed to it. I never succeeded, however, in getting to any clear conception of it till I had come to see in aesthetics a cognitive activity, and till I had come to recognise a clear distinction between pure and applied aesthetics. This distinction is the subject of the present chapter.

Pure and applied aesthetics are very different from fine art and applied art. These are conventional terms to which no clear meaning can be attached, as the difference is partly functional, partly a social estimate of "uselessness," and partly an ideal valuation. The difference between pure and applied aesthetics depends upon there being some fairly precise meaning of the word *applied*. Since *applied* does not mean *put on* but *used for*, or practical, we shall have to consider what meaning can be found for the word *practical*.

It needs no elaborate demonstration to show that the usual meaning of the word *practical* is too narrow for exact use. The word commonly refers to economic benefits of the kind that are recognised by the community. To the man, for instance, who *really* believed that the most valuable treasures are laid up in heaven, one who by preference laid them up on earth would seem lacking in practical good sense. Practicality must be given a definition that includes all its forms, it must refer to what is involved in them all. This character is, I think, the consumption, immediate or postponed, of goods. Consumption is related closely to the transitoriness of the instrumental, of which so much was made in a previous chapter. To deal practically is to look forward to consumption. The cognitive activity is not practical, because its goal is never consumption, but indefinitely continued production. It may lead to consumption, and often does, but to reach this state there must be a change of direction. The subject of this chapter is the consumption that is involved in many of the satisfactions, sometimes explicit satisfactions, in aesthetic facts.

Before I begin the discussion of this, I shall give an illustration of the two conditions of aesthetic experience. There hangs before me on the wall the reproduction of a Chinese landscape. It is typically, for me, a picture that I look into and keep out of. I find it essentially complete. I am so well satisfied when I look at it that I do not think of the satisfaction at all. When I am positively interested in it, that is, when I am not partially thinking of something else, I continue to explore it, and in so doing I intensify it. It has proved, so far, a field for indefinitely continued exploration.

In contrast with this, take a fox-trot that I was playing on the gramophone a little while ago. It was, musically speaking, a rather poor fox-trot, and while I listened to it I had a strong impulse to act it out, to complete it, as it were, by dancing to it. When however, I determinedly listened to it as though it were musically sufficient, it seemed to have empty and meaningless spaces. One could complete it by dancing, or by sentimentalising, or if one had the necessary ability, by rewriting it. In all these cases there is something further done than just the knowing it. The object is not a mere cognitive object, but it is material to be used in making something else. Such an object is not capable of standing by itself, and is not, for the person who feels that way about it, a pure aesthetic object.

Pure aesthetic experience except as a momentary flash is rare. This is the case because there are very few people who can for any length of time keep up the cognitive interest. Almost everyone is interested in bits, in odds and ends, of science, but very few can hold their attention long enough to accumulate the knowledge which is needed for the understanding of a complicated system, unless they have a further motive. Plenty of people rejoice in what knowledge they believe themselves to possess, but very few possess much of it accurately, outside of their occupational range. They are generally in too great a hurry to use it, often in ways that we do not usually think of as practical. Knowledge may be used to augment one's self-feeling—"He put in his thumb and he pulled out a plum, and said, what a bright boy am I." There are many persons who cannot sustain interest in knowledge unless they are permitted to run out every few minutes to tell their neighbours what they have learned. In all such cases their interest is as practical, even if not as useful, as though they were learning to build a house, or run a truck farm. Day-dreaming is a practical interest purely, though its practicality is a pseudo-practicality, and thoroughly futile. It is a way of turning all experience into an immediately available form by a fanciful circumvention of time, space, and matter. Concerning the practical, as for so many other things in studies like ours, understanding can come only by cutting directly across the categories of common sense.

It may be objected that the cognitive theory of the pure aesthetic does not fit the facts, since there is the marked tendency to return again and again, to the object, and the purer the experience is in aesthetic quality, the more is this so. We return to a story less often than to a poem, to a poem less often than to a piece of music or a picture. The less there is to know, apparently, the more frequent is the perusal.

The paradox comes out clearly enough in that last sentence. Is it true that there is less to know where the presumed thing to be known is less tangible? I do not think so. The trouble comes with the conception of knowing, which we usually take in a special and rather narrow sense. We usually ignore the stages of getting to know, as part of the process, and only consider the thing as known when it is quite clear. But in doing this we neglect much of what happens.

When we have learned a clear-cut fact, we henceforth either know it or do not know it. If we have occasion to refer to it and cannot accurately recall it, we look it up, that is, we re-acquire it. But, many times, our facts are not so clear as this. We have knowledge of a shade of colour, or some quality of an object that we cannot precisely define, which we keep available by "keeping our hand, or eye, in." We have in such cases to do with things that we cannot learn once for all, but which have to be continually relearned more or less. The relearning is not as in the first instance a re-acquisition of that which has been lost, but is rather a refurbishing, a restoration of that which tends to lose its distinctness. Certain skilled capacities are very fluctuant, and therefore prestidigitators, dancers and musical performers, lose their certainty very quickly if their practice is intermitted. It is not merely a matter of flexibility, but of the precisely right adjustment. They must know exactly what to do, though of course the knowledge is not of an abstract sort.

In aesthetics we have to do with complex wholes which are never in a state of rigid adjustment. To know them once and for all is impossible, unless they are of a kind to which we can attach little importance. It is only when the aesthetic object is one that we have surpassed, that we regard it as finally known. There are many who regard Longfellow as known, but very few think that way of Shakespeare. In rereading, or even in reading, Longfellow, they are likely to have the feeling of a mere recall. What they get is no more than what they expected. Of course, if they could in some way get the necessary interest, they might find out that there was more in it. So it often happens that outworn art is renewed because a new interest is developed, and that in consequence, people want to know things that before had not occurred to them. But the main point, I think, is clear. Without something to know in the renewal of the experience, aesthetic activity loses its specific object, and becomes applied, applied, that is, to something else than that object.

People have no idea how slight is their capacity for sustained looking at works of art. They pass through galleries looking at one picture after another, rarely stopping long enough to see anything more than what they are prepared to see at a glance. It would do them little good to stop longer, for their interest is exhausted when they have seen so much. If they are compelled to more deliberation, they think about something else, which may be connected with the work of art, but which has nothing to do with its aesthetic character. If they are curious about it, their concern may be with its historical associations, its subject matter, its technique, or critical ideas about it, but more probably they go off on trains of sentimental thought, or else they turn to definitely emotional satisfactions.

Emotion in aesthetic experience gets a simple explanation when it is taken as something that does not belong to the cognitive experience at all except through association with an emotionally charged memory, but which is a consequence of that experience that can heighten it by reaction. When the emotion becomes primary, the attention has been partly turned away from that object. I have already said that I consider emotion to be a massive feeling related to the viscera and glands, which is devoid of particular colour or character. It is one expression of the tension produced within the body system. After an impression has been taken in at the eyes, for instance, the tension continues to other parts of the skeletal musculature, and may go on to involve the viscera. It is possible that this commonly happens more or less, but it need not attract the attention away from the visual object. In ordinary happenings it does not even colour the object, which remains neutrally related within the utilitarian situation. An emotion, if it is commonly aroused, which is questionable, is hardly more than a by-product.

Emotion is a kind of resonator that amplifies feeling, amplifies perceptive intensity. Under usual conditions one does not pay attention to the amplifier but only to that which is increased. But one may cease to pay attention to the speech or the music, and be interested only in the volume of noise. So it is with emotion. Something analogous is true of feeling and even of perception, when the personal application is intrusive. Some people are incapable of sticking to the point, and are always running off into those personal applications under the mistaken notion that therein lies the essence of the argument. A crude form of this is the intrusion of a "But that is not the way that I do it," into an objective situation. People that have this habit look upon "the way that they do it," as an integral element in the habits of the Tonga islanders, or of the moral situation of their neighbours. The diversion of interest to feelings that do not belong there, or to emotion that is essentially neuter, is the same kind of thing.

A clear distinction must be made between emotional enhancement, and satisfaction in emotion. When emotions are attended to as sources of satisfaction, the aesthetic object has really become a factory of emotions, which are thereupon consumed. When the duke in *Twelfth Night* says,

> *If music be the food of love, play on;*
> *Give me excess of it, that surfeiting, the*
> *appetite may sicken, and so die,*

he means that he wants through music such an emotional debauch, that for the time being he will be full-fed and incapable of more. As soon as the music ceases to be effectual, he orders it to stop. There is a world of difference between satisfaction in the emotion, and satisfaction in the thing from which emotion is derived. The duke may very well have been a connoisseur and may have preferred good music, but "that dying fall" for which he asked again, did not produce the desired emotional effect and he wanted no more of it, no matter how good it was. It is indifferent whether the consumable emotion is coarse or refined, whether it is called an aesthetic emotion or anything else; if the object is dissolved in the emotion rather than the emotion in the object, we have to do with a practical utilisation of an aesthetic object.

It would be a great mistake to draw from this distinction the inference that suppression of the emotion is desirable. Quite the contrary. The more freely one laughs at what one finds funny or weeps over what one finds sad, the more easily that one expands with what relaxes and contracts with what restricts, the less is one likely to be troubled by one's emotions, if one's interest is in the object. If instead, one likes emotional indulgence, and has that as his principal interest, giving way to it will not make the experience more genuinely aesthetic.

Emotions are almost never real objects of an aesthetic experience. They are too vague and unformed to be taken as objects of knowledge. Indeed the effect of attending to one's emotions is commonly to destroy the purity of such an object. One can with difficulty have the object and the emotion also. By stressing the emotion one puts the object out of focus, for when one uses the object as an emotional factory, one relates it to oneself in ways that are irrelevant to its intrinsic constitution. The object has been made through the feelings, but when one then relates it to one's resultant feelings and emotions, one deprives it of the measure of freedom that one has endowed it with. It is like the case of the father who gives the child money to do with as it likes with the proviso that the money must be put in the bank. To the thing is first given an individual rhythm, which is then perverted to other uses.

I said a moment ago that aesthetic interest is not often kept up for a long time, and that people almost always pass rapidly through art galleries. There is nothing that they look at for a long time without being expectant, inventorial, or sentimental. They can watch a fisherman for hours in the hope of seeing him catch a fish. They can look at a landscape, noting this or that. They can moon quite endlessly, whether there is a moon to help them or not. Under these conditions they may feel aesthetically active. Goethe in the beginning of Werther's sorrows, gives an excellent picture of a man mooning, and feeling himself an artist. I give a condensed translation of the passage. "I am so happy, so entirely absorbed in the feeling of my tranquil existence, that my art suffers by it. I could not draw a single stroke now, but I have never been a greater artist than at these moments … . When the sun rests on the impenetrable obscurity of my forest, and only single rays steal into my sanctuary … when I note the teeming life of the little world among the grass blades … when I feel the presence of the Almighty who created us in His image, the breath of the All-loving who sustains us floating in eternal bliss … when all that dawns before my eyes, and when the world about me and the heavens sink into my soul like the form of a beloved, then am I filled with longing and I think: If only thou couldst express that, if thou couldst breathe onto the paper what lies in thee so full and warm, so that it should become the mirror of thy soul as thy soul is the mirror of the infinite God! But I go to pieces under this, I am overcome by the immensity of splendour of this pageant."

Werther was much mistaken when he thought that he was at these moments a great artist. An artist is one who turns outward and not inward, unless he turns himself inward outward. Werther was looking eagerly at the varied spectacle before him, moving from one thrilling item to another, but the whole that he realised was not the whole of the spectacle but a whole of personal feeling. The artist is not distinguished either by the quality or the amount of his feeling, but by the intensity and comprehensiveness of his unifying perception. He must be able to look long and hard. His seeing must also be cumulative. He learns to see just as other persons learn any other subject. His special technical studies affect his mode of seeing, but the essential thing common to all aesthetic activity which amounts to something, is the capacity to maintain the objective interest long enough to master the material and so to put it into form. This is true whether one is an artist or a spectator. Those who cannot find in themselves the interest to do this, will never get far in their aesthetic development. They will be expectant, inventorial, or sentimental. If sufficiently endowed, like Werther, they will be all these things at once.

Expectancy belongs to aesthetics as a character in rhythmic movement, but expectancy in a detective story is generally something else. As the story is usually written, the interest depends upon the desired solution. The reader's sympathy is either with the criminal, or the detective, or some innocent victim. Rarely, as in the *Murder in the Rue Morgue*, or in *The Gold-Bug*, is the interest purely in the story, in the inherent logic or rhythm. Where the success or failure of the hero is the vital interest, sympathy with him, or even closer identification, is the source of satisfaction. The state of affairs is the same as with the gallery gods of the old melodrama, as with the lovers of a happy ending in the movies or the drama, or with the demand for poetic justice in the older tragedy. In all these cases the conclusion is something more than the working out of the theme. It is necessary that as an end it should be the result that the spectators want. The aesthetic object is only transient for them at the best; more usually it is perverted in order to meet their demand for personal and particular satisfaction.

In general it takes a very highly civilised person to be satisfied with no other measure of expectancy in aesthetic experience than the working out of the implicit logic or rhythm. Most persons consider such an attitude as inhuman or immoral. They are incapable of distinguishing between doing and knowing, and consider it immoral to know what they consider it improper to do. Of course they are not consistent in the sort of thing, and manage furtively, or by insisting in one way or another that it is dreadful, to have to listen to such things, to listen to as much of it as they can get. But when they set out with a fair good conscience, and with entire openness, to satisfy their aesthetic impulses, they demand that expectancy shall sweeten life, and that the rhythm shall be infantile, or shall be perverted. Of course those who dislike the rose-coloured, and who insist that all real experience is ugly, do the same kind of thing with another objective. Both the sweet Pollyanna tale and the gruesome tale of morbid realism might have their genuine rhythm, but neither does usually have it, and neither is central in human experience. What is desired, is in another class from that which is aesthetically pure. Here the point is the difference between expectation as a principal interest, and expectation as an interest in the development of the thematic material. Whether we have to do with music, literature, or painting, this distinction is applicable.

I have mentioned three forms of aesthetic perversion—the expectant, the inventorial, the sentimental. The inventorial perversion is largely due to the fact, already mentioned, that people cannot maintain the cognitive attitude long without enquiring into particulars. An artist can work for years at a statue without elaborating details. The figure when it is finished may look to the inexperienced eye like a sketch done in a few days. Merely patient workers can, on the other hand, work endlessly in elaborating. The detail, if it is kept within the terms of the rhythmic whole, is, of course, no fault. But such conditions are the exception. Usually the elaborations take the place of an aesthetic coherence which the artist cannot achieve, and act as a substitute.

We can recur here to the distinction that I made between art that is good for advertising, and art that is not. In the one case we are to become partakers, and in the other we remain observers. The observer of a single thing remains in a single place spiritually, even if there is psychological or physical displacement. We may pass through a poem or a sonata, or go round a building or a statue, without a displacement in our meaning attitude. But to do this requires effort. Therefore people's impressions of wholes are usually vague, and only particulars are distinct. No one who is not specially interested in such matters has any idea how rarely the reader of a book knows what is in it, or how rarely the critic is in contact with his subject matter.

It is much easier to take the aesthetic object piecemeal than to take it wholly. I have spoken of the importance of breaking up the inward-running lines of a picture so as to make of them rhythmic series, rather than fluent directions. Otherwise it happens that one travels inward never to return. If the lines are broken but not rhythmically, one takes the lines in sections with successive bits of scenery, but here again there is not the rhythmic throw-back to the frontal plane which maintains the continuity and unity of expression. It is rare indeed for composition in depth to be really good, and I find a confirmation of my analysis in the fact that those pictures which seemed to be formally most complete before I had thought of this way of taking them, conform most closely to the conditions of my present statement. I came to the matter by trying to understand how a painter sees, and the result seems to show that by this method one can really attain the desired end.

Many persons cannot find a lasting interest in a picture unless they can run around in it, touch the things represented, and hear the people talk or at least see them do something. For such persons the pure aesthetic situation hardly exists, but applied aesthetics is a source of real satisfaction.

The last form of aesthetic application is the sentimental. This differs from the expectant chiefly because it refers to a present state rather than to a future one. Expectancy is often sentimental in nature, but one can as well be sentimental in the present. This means that we are looking at the object as though it referred to us when it is, in fact, utterly unconcerned about us. I once used the illustration of infinity to show how an extended scene can make the spectator feel infinite, can make him feel as though he were climbing up the ladder of nature to touch the stars. Critical objectivity is very unpopular, especially with the realistic man of common sense. He is so in the habit of intruding his ego into every situation with which he comes in contact, that this seems to him the normal condition of objectivity. His predilections, his possessive impulses, his bumptious intrusiveness, make the world real to him. The purity of aesthetic experience is, except for fleeting moments, as remote from the range of his interests as are all the other conditions of a life that does not give him a central place.

The sentimentality of the realist, in this sense, is matched by the sentimentality of the dreamer, who regards all that is objective as an interruption of his fantasy life. His relation to pure aesthetic experience is the same as that of the overtly practical man. The chief difference is that the "realist" is more social, in the economic-political sense of the word, and that therefore his adaptation of aesthetic experience to his ends has more publicity than that of the shyer sentimentality of the dreamer. The one is a Babbitt, the other an inhabitant of Fairyland. The one inscribes his sentimentalities upon a banner; the other on an inward palimpsest. The one says "we" and shares in every glory; the other whispers "I" in secret, and envies the glorious one. Sentimentality is the pervading vice of a humanity not at one with itself, and in a world of such, pure aesthetic experience has very little place. The practical need of making life seem coherent when in fact it isn't, destroys the possibility of sustainedly honest relations between a man and his possible experience.

It remains to speak of aesthetics in relation to science. Science, as has been so often repeated, concerns itself with propositions, and aesthetics with pictures. Most people prefer pictures to propositions, and what serves them as science is in large part pictorial. Their notion of the solar system is rather a moving picture of balls rolling round a luminous ball in the centre, than of masses related to each other according to Newton's laws of motion. It is striking, if one has ever had occasion to note it, how people can have the belief of a perfect understanding of scientific facts, without being able, if called upon, to make any intelligible statement of them. Their impression is something like that which they might have of a country concerning which they express opinions, but about which they can say nothing that has a definite meaning.

It is not only true that Everyman's science is unscientific, but it is equally true that he cannot remain with it long even as something to become acquainted with pictorially. He soon wants to turn it to account. This is equally true when the material does not lend itself to industrial purposes. Many people read enthusiastically about relativity, but soon abandon the effort to get clear ideas of the relations that it asserts. They fall back upon relatedness as in itself thrilling, but this interest cannot last very long. The next step and the fated one, is to go on to God, Freedom, and Immortality. Even science becomes tolerable when it is so brought to the service of man. That is the normal progression of pure science, of science that is not industrially applicable, in the popular mind.

I have not mentioned the distinction between fine art and applied art, because no distinction is possible. It has been sufficiently made evident that fine art is usually applied in a number of ways. In differentiating fine art and applied art, the intention is usually to separate off art which is related to industry. As long as we stick to actual utensils as different from lyric poetry, the matter is simple, but when we come to vases that are made to look at but which are too precious to hold anything, the distinction gets lost. In a final chapter on Art (Chapter XXII) I shall give some of the numerous reasons why the distinction besides being impossible, is objectionable.

It may be worthwhile, however, to point out how usefulness may become an aesthetic character when it is taken as the quality of a thing. In a chair I may perceive a certain rhythm, a beauty of form, and I may say that it is not only beautiful but that it is comfortable as well. Instead of making this separation I might see in the comfortableness an added quality of the chair which makes it, aesthetically speaking, a different kind of thing from a chair which is beautiful but not comfortable. In a case like this, comfort is taken as a feeling of which the chair becomes a symbolic expression. Of course it is not the expression of this feeling alone. In that, however, it is not peculiar, since almost all aesthetic objects are, as symbols, complex.

It is possible that a reader of this chapter gets an impression that derogating from the loftiness of pure aesthetic knowing, and using aesthetic objects for other purposes, is reprehensible. This is, of course, not at all my meaning. This matter must be given its full discussion later, but I can say here that in respect of such things, whatever is, is right. There is no use eating what one cannot digest. There is no use trying to satisfy a demand which does not exist. In order that people should take much interest in knowing, they must have their more intimate needs, in some fair measure, satisfied. A man will not, except from necessity, keep quiet when he is restless. He will not abstain from vain dreams unless his effort is sustained by some promise of realising his desires. The first condition of sustained pure aesthetic interest is that people should have time for this, and have learned that the result is really valuable.

All this apart, applied aesthetics is just as legitimate as that which is pure. The great spiritual evil is confusion. Therefore if one knows what one is doing, there is no spiritual harm in doing it. There is no harm in travelling about in a painted landscape. There is no harm in sharing the emotions of one's favourite hero or heroine. Sometimes we take interest in bits of beauty on the way, and in any case reading sentimental literature or sentimentally looking at nature and art would, if it were done knowingly, be just a form of clowning. The finer aesthetic tact and less repressed erotic temper of the Latins have led them to invent sentimental clowns in the form of Pierrot and Pierrette and Harlequin. Anglo-Saxony has not gotten so far as this, and therefore has produced the largest mass of sentimental slush that the world has ever known.

The distinction between pure and applied aesthetics is of central importance as the social-aesthetic problem, but before recurring to it in a concluding chapter on Art (Chapter XXII), we shall have to make a pause, while we consider the place of cognitive experience in general and of the aesthetic experience in particular, in the course of experience as a whole.

XIX. Aesthetic Experience as Knowledge

WE HAVE SO FAR been concerned to find out as exactly as possible what was meant by the aesthetic experience, and in this chapter we shall examine the value of the experience. If it is essentially an act of knowing, then its importance must eventually depend on the importance of the thing known. Science is important because it gives knowledge of structure and function throughout the realm of experienced things. Aesthetics which makes us acquainted with the world as it is organically related to ourselves, cannot give us anything more important than can be constituted by the selves. This is equally true, of course, for creation and for appreciation. We must therefore give some attention to the value of selves, and their role in the life of the individual.

Selves have almost unlimited possibilities of development provided that they can continue to assimilate experience. In common practice they do nothing of the kind. They get themselves arrested early in life, either in the trammels of neurotic fixations, the so-called complexes, or in the conventions of social life. The physical sciences have after ages of struggle fairly freed themselves from this kind of arrest, the biological sciences have almost reached freedom, and the psychological sciences are on the way. The result of this kind of emancipation is a stock of knowledge which will eventually prevent the formation of complexes, with their consequence of self-formations that cannot loosen up in order to avail themselves of what might be learned. But this goal is very, very, remote. For the present we can discuss the whole matter as an almost academic question. Taking it in that way we have to make certain assumptions. One assumption is that human experience is in some practicable sense real. It need not be really real, for the universe may be able to get along without it, and perhaps did so for a long time. Therefore it may be entirely unwarranted to use the kind of intelligence that human beings possess, as an instrument for metaphysically explaining the universe. Human intelligence may be an evolutionary product which is entirely incommensurable with absolute intelligence, if there is any such thing. We may never know anything except in terms of our acquaintance with things, and that may be limited. The kind of reality that I assume, therefore, is the practicable reality of experience into which we dive in the pursuit of knowledge, and to which we return with the knowledge acquired.

The other assumption is that selves are instrumental, that they are means for elaborating experience, and that they are made by the contact of the individual with things, some of which are necessarily other individuals outside the first one. The scientific experience has a standard of value unrelated to the self, otherwise than as the self is capable of apprehending relations, but the aesthetic experience in its authentic character is strictly limited by the development of the self, through which it is produced. By assimilating a certain social habit, by developing analogies, by being critical, in short, one can make a kind of aesthetic self that serves well enough for a limited round of appreciations within the world of art, but which has next to nothing to do with the larger field that I have spoken of as the whole aesthetic range. As I care nothing whatever for the "fine arts" as a superior kind of thing which people should be interested in, I cannot regard this critically developed sensibility as having any great importance. It seems to me exactly on a par with a refined taste in wines or cigars. The two things often go together. My concern is not at all with this aesthetic self, but with other and more important ones. The self is modified by knowledge. It changes by acquisition. The process of knowing is not a process of acquiring the objects known, but it is indubitably a process of acquiring knowledge of them. It assumes that the objects exist and can be known. It makes no difference whether they come entirely from the outside, or from the inside. They may be objects in "nature," or they may be mental creations that have grown from the mind's preceding activities. In any case they are now there to be discovered. As I said before, whether an answer is found to a problem posed long in advance, or which has just been posed, or even has never been explicitly posed, it is actually discovered and in some sense, therefore, has been existent. The object is not altered by being known, but the knower is. Since this is the case, we shall have to be at some pains to make it clear how there is a knowing in the event of aesthetic experience.

That in science there is an acquisition of knowledge is obvious. Its products are ideas which one comes to possess, and which can be salted away for further reference. What one knows, one knows. But one returns to a picture again and again as though one had taken from it nothing except an impression. The learner approaches as something new, that which for others are known facts in science, but there does not seem to be in aesthetics any clear analogy to this. There does not seem to be any definite terminus to the knowing process.

My own experience says that there is. Whenever I look at a picture, listen to music, or read a poem, while really attending to it, that is, while I am abstaining from all the acts that I have called applied aesthetics, I find myself gathering together the things—the inventorial elements of line, colour, subject-matter, or what is analogous in the other arts—and getting to know them. Of course the process is not carried out inventorially, though there is much specific notation, the more if the thing is radically unfamiliar, or strikingly different from what is usual. In similar wise, if a painter asks me to look critically at his work, I find that I have to search a lot before I find anything to say that I feel justified in saying.

People have commonly no idea how little they see of a picture, or of the aesthetic aspect of anything. They are unaware that their seeing is largely conventional, that they are habitually looking at some *kind* of thing rather than at some *particular* thing, and that therefore anyone who knows their taste can easily say beforehand what they will like. If a person's perception is the result of really seeking for the qualities of the thing presented, this is impossible. At all events, people often have told me that I would like this or that because I had liked something that seemed to them similar, or that I would dislike it for some equally good reason, when it turned out upon trial that I did nothing of the kind. For purposes of applied aesthetics these group judgments are good enough. If one is really interested in one's emotions, then it may well happen that some kind of a thing will set them off; or if one is a radical or a conservative, a realist or an idealist, a humanist or a diabolist, or belongs to any of the innumerable sects that swarm wherever art is cultivated, it may well be sufficient that the given object is of the kind demanded, and is not too obviously bad. But if one wants really to see the thing before one, one must do something more than glance at it. I cannot, I know, see a picture till I have looked at it for some time, till I have brought its parts to a stable adjustment, until I have made of them a whole. I do not think that it is sufficient to accept the hint that the kind of thing that it seems to be is the thing that it is going to be, nor can I be hasty to accept the absence of obviously successful organisation, as evidence that the object has none. I believe that a serious artist of even small abilities puts more into a canvas than anyone can see in a moment. It is remarkable how often a painter "is discovered," after hundreds of people have seen his work again and again, after they have written about it, apparently without having *seen* it, and how they all see it as soon as it has been discovered. The number of "masterpieces" is much smaller than the textbooks would lead one to think, but the number of pictures that have some real merit is very large. It is convenient, of course, to schematise all this sort of thing, but it belongs to the same class of meaningless abbreviations as the conventional traits of Frenchmen or Britishers, of Philadelphians or Bostonians.

When I have once really seen a picture—I shall go on in the first person as I dislike the absurd practice by which one pretends to speak for all the world when one really speaks only for oneself—I find that it is often finished for me. It is not because I am tired of it, or have gotten beyond that kind of thing, but simply that I am so well acquainted with it that looking cannot go beyond recognition. The thing has gotten to have a sort of diagrammatic fixity which prevents the parts from being really confluent, one with another. This finality of formal character is the death of the aesthetic object.

It often happens that after I have seen a picture quite completely, as it seems to me, I return to it and find it, so to speak, unpossessed. I have more or less forgotten it and must once more go through the process of seeing it. As long as the picture has any real interest for me as pure aesthetic value, I find a continuing need of re-forming it. As the picture gets to be better known, this happens more easily, and in most cases, the time comes when nothing more can be done about it, unless some new interest leads me to look at the picture in a different way. Apart from that, the work can now serve only for applied aesthetic purposes, for comfort, stimulation, emotional luxury, sentimental revery, or it can remain as a recorded fact, an item, a moment in my biography.

As long as it happens that what I call applied aesthetics is taken as making for the chief values of art, all that I am saying will seem rather insignificant. But as I have already said, we are confronted with the paradox of the serious interest in art as a social function, and the frivolity of our particular attitudes regarding it. Current theories of aesthetics as emotional satisfaction, as compensation, and all that sort of thing, justify the frivolity, but they do not justify the seriousness otherwise than as art is one of the minor industries, like safety-razors, for instance, or cosmetics. In order to get beyond that, we have to get into the other field.

People in general are so little conscious of pure aesthetics because they have so little share in it. Their contacts with works of art which are their only explicit occasions for aesthetic experience, are almost always made for the purpose of getting on to enjoyment of one kind or another, either emotional satisfactions, or the satisfaction of having opinions about them, that they hardly know what the pure experience is like. Yet the decisive importance lies with the pure and not the applied forms. That is the interest which stimulates the artist to reach after something that the layman is hardly aware of. He knows that the artist ought to show an integrity, that he ought to deliver his "message" without flinching from the "truth," but what all this is about, he does not know. He usually takes this to mean that the artist should not lie about social fact, and that he should not commercialise his work. He should work to satisfy himself, and not to satisfy the public. But after all, if the public does not genuinely partake of that which the artists have made, why should it be solicitous about the artist's aesthetic morality?

The genuine interest of the public and that of the artist are identical. Neither is concerned with truth in the sense of making a statement about something, but both are, or would be if they had a pure interest, concerned about fact. The report of the aesthetic observer is analogous to that of the naturalist who has been in a new country and brings back an account of the animals and plants there. He must not fake the report. The first demand made of him is that he should be honest. After that we can demand competence. He should see accurately, but also widely and deeply. The artist's field is the world seen through the self. That is his subject matter. His form, that which should give to this subject matter an existential self-subsisting reality, is the rhythmic whole. The type of rhythm may itself indicate the subject, but its wholeness makes its expressional competence.

The observer who takes art as something more than a luxury, has to do the same thing that the artist has done, except that the dirty work of pioneering has been done for him. If there is no special importance which attaches to the aesthetic discovery, then I am quite unable to see why there is any special importance that is characteristic of good art as opposed to bad, except what is characteristic of any kind of goods. If we pay more for them we expect them to last longer, or to look better, or to work more effectually, than if we put up with a cheaper sort. The aesthetic object can in any case be subject to these demands, but if we ask more than this, then what is further demanded can be grounded rationally only upon a superior importance of service. There is this importance, in the possible development of the self due to the expressive significance of aesthetic experience. The self and its growth are the central underlying themes when we look for the grounds of the imputed importance of the aesthetic. A word more in conclusion of the present subject, and we shall have to turn to the self.

The peculiar value of an aesthetic object for the pure experience comes to an end when there is nothing more to be discovered. This happens when the quality is felt as mere reminiscence. To rediscover it is to see it with intense objectivity, as one sees a friend who has been absent a long time, or as one sees a person to whom one is attached, whose health is occasion for anxiety. One tries to see into him, to note changes in him, in short one tries to reknow him. When there is nothing to see or when there is no curiosity, the person becomes a mere recognition-object, one that is identified for reasons of convenience or pleasure.

The interest in the aesthetic as an acquisition of knowledge is incompatible with the current ideas of classics in art. The tendency is to regard classics as given for all time, as something one should be connected with if one can as with the best families, as standards, as models of aesthetic deportment. In fact, the classics taken in this way, are, for pure aesthetics, of the least possible importance. They are valuable, if rightly taken because they, in general, last longer. They are instances of the intensest seeing most successfully expressed. Consequently they have the capacity, in a superior degree, of inducing the attitude of rediscovery. But though their expression in symbol, of the felt values, is more precise and richer than that of other works, the difference does not give to them any absolute values. A classic becomes a mere fetish when it is considered other than a field for discovery, or an object of use or amusement. It then turns into something like Poole's label on one's overcoat, or Paquin's on one's dress. It becomes the symbolic expression of an aesthetic self, existing for its own sake as a peculiar value. This dissociates art from the rest of life, and makes, if not art for art's sake, at least art for the sake of being artistic. This kind of thing is the basis of museums, or art collections, of lectures on art, and all the rest of the tedious business of making art important. It is radically inconsistent with that which I consider the basic value of the aesthetic experience—its capacity to serve for the unification of the self, to make knowledge of the self available, and consequently to further its development. From this point of view everything which makes for aesthetic objects that are too good for use, is a perversion of them.

XX. Selves

O RGANISMS ARE SELF-PRESERVATIVE, AND they endure in a variety of relations to each other, and to other things. However, a group of organisms, even if closely related, does not constitute a society. In order that the social condition should be attained, it is necessary that the group should have an organic structure in which stability of function should exist with a mobility of the individual members. If the society is to be flexible and adapted to varied conditions, there must be a correlative freedom of communication, and a consequent growth of intelligence. Societies are associations in which intelligence is possible, and in the long run, effective intelligence is the important thing in a society.

Intelligence can exist only with communication, and whatever limits communication limits intelligence. There was a time when scientists kept their secrets to themselves, and gave out only hints and carefully abridged statements. Progress was correspondingly slow. In some cases it has happened that valuable information was not published because it had never reached the stage of necessary completeness. In other cases, as in the notable ones of Mendel and Gibbs, the publication was made where those qualified to use it did not come upon it, and it was necessary for them to do the work over again later. Much valuable time was in this way lost. Today, however, scientific communication is thoroughgoing, to the great advantage of science.

Human society is made up of individuals who know themselves and are known to others as selves, but the conditions of that society do not encourage any high degree of publicity in the knowledge of the selves. There is a certain eagerness to know about others, but even this curiosity is tempered by a measure of identification with related individuals, which would tend to make us know ourselves in knowing the others. The more remote the individual being studied, the more possibility there is of frankness and thoroughness. Anthropology has meant to most people the study of other races, preferably inferior ones. Everyone has heard the story of the American lady who assured Freud that *such* things might be true of Austrians but that Americans were different. I have seen statements of the same kind, made by French doctors.

The self-preservative tendency of the individual does not make for any high degree of social intelligence. In this respect society is still in the condition of medieval science. Every man is interested in making the best possible appearance, and he has no interest at all in being known for what he really is. Nor is it desirable that he should know himself since in that case he would have to play a part whenever he appears in public. It is much more desirable that he should believe a fiction, and profit by the increase of power that the belief gives him. The consequence is a society that is at war within itself in a thousand ways, and which is therefore condemned to barbarism.

I think that it may well happen, if the world ever becomes civilised, that Sigmund Freud will be recognised as the man that laid civilisation's cornerstone by making the first serious breach in the ostrich policy of humankind. He was the first who took upon himself the opprobrium of being completely veracious, or, if not quite that, of being much more veracious than anyone had thought of being before except in the demi-disguise of literature. He has put upon a solid basis the factual side of the self-complication, not merely that of the explicit neurotic, but that of the so-called normal man as well. It is upon the ground of the sort of fact that he has rendered familiar, that any intelligible treatment of aesthetics is possible.

The self I have defined in a former chapter as a product of the intersection of lines of awareness running into, and running out from, the subject. For each individual there are innumerable selves depending upon a multitude of relations. Some of these are merely conveniences which are recognised as artifices as when we play with children or pay a ceremonial visit, but the greater part, and the more important ones, are not so easily put on and off. Most of our selves we are obliged to defend to a greater or less extent, and whatever we are obliged to defend, we must surrender to more or less. We lose a certain measure of our liberty with every such obligation that we assume, and with it a portion of our privilege to be intelligent. There may be some compensation as when Catholic philosophers were prevented from being critical about foundations and became correspondingly acute in dialectic. But the loss is greater than the gain.

As long as a man remains a group of selves that is more or less confused, that has incomprehensible rigidities, and helpless contradictions, he will be ineffectual in his relations to the knowledge which depends upon his selves. A man may be an excellent scientist under such conditions because science has standards outside the range of the self, and he may be a good artist or a good critic within certain limits, because he identifies someone of his selves as his *truth* and finds expression through it. If, however, one asks of aesthetic expression a more significant service than just to be somebody's utterance, if one demands of it that it should be related to an organic growth in civilisation, if, that is, one is to take it as something to be judged otherwise than with the eccentricity of a self-assertive self-imposed judge, then it will have to be referred to a more dependable authority than any that we can at present find.

This authority is the unified self. The condition of its existence is publicity. It is necessary not only that we should know about ourselves, that is, that we should have studied psychology, but that we should know ourselves. This is not impossible even if we evade actual publicity, but on this condition it is so difficult, as to be impracticable. But if the time should ever come when through an extension of psychological knowledge we should reach the point that we could not and would not avoid knowing all our thoughts and their implications—for repression has to do with thought primarily and not action—then there would concurrently come the possibility of a thorough socialisation. People would cease to live in the terrible solitude of their self-defensive mendacity, and civilisation would be on the way.

If we had come to this, we could break down the present distinction in respect of aesthetics, of art and life. At present when art is compensatory or else related chiefly to that wretched little aesthetic self, it is remote from life and stands in contrast with it. But if the self was unified in the sense that all the selves were confluent, if the momentary selves for different occasions were only diverted currents of the main stream, then the aestheticism of the customary sort would have its true character of a game, and would be distinguished from the pure aesthetic experience, which would be the parts of real existence seen through the self and treated as real. Then aesthetics could be taken as that form of knowledge by which we grasp organic wholes and make them humanly intelligible.

It could be plausibly objected that a picture of reality taken as such would not necessarily have the rhythmic character of a fully expressed aesthetic object, and that therefore there is a contradiction in the notion that there can be an adequate aesthetic view of life. I do not think that this objection would hold, for it ignores the distinction between the thing to be expressed and the expression of it. An expression is always to some extent a translation which brings to its fullest value some aspect of a situation. The ability of the observer or artist to make it apparent in a form that serves the intended end is shown in his capacity to make the object self-existent, or simply, to make it an object.

An important consequence of the unified self and the resultant interrelation of the objects of the intermittent selves, would be a tendency to make of living activities objects that are aesthetically acceptable. Whenever we make a picture, we begin by composing the things upon which it is based. I have shown that a well-arranged group of things will not necessarily make a good picture, but a good picture is more easily made with a well-posed model. So it would be with our aesthetic perception of the material world in which we live. We would have a much stronger impulse to make that world beautiful, if it were habitually seen. It can, however, come to be seen only on the condition that the world of selves becomes a public world, that its objects become genuinely public objects, and that intelligent action is not barred because of the more or less pathological self-defence that the disintegrated selves set up.

An important result of self-integration would be a change in our attitude toward artists. Today the artist is a privileged outcast in the world. He is something between the honest workman and the public ward. His talent is his excuse. We are supposed to look at his pictures and read his books no matter how mad we think him, provided that he is a genius. He is obligated to a certain integrity, which does not mean that he should see truly, but that he should truly tell what he sees. Since the aesthetic interest is cut off from the interests of the self in its other relations, criticism of the artist, except as a genius, is considered irrelevant.

The difference between the censor and the aesthete is that the former takes the position that art is related to life in general, and the latter takes the position that it is not. It is rather a curious state of affairs. The censor is stupidly right on the main issue, and the aesthete is intelligently wrong. In a world of diffused intelligence there could be no question. In such a world it would be seen that *everything* should be known, even the facts about sex and the perversities of artists. Repression of knowledge would be seen as incompetent to solve any problem. On the other hand, aesthetic experience would not be an occasional curiosity, and therefore the crippled genius would lose his importance. Aesthetic objects would be taken in course, and what is tainted would be rejected as tainted meat is by those whose appetite is not strong for that kind of thing. Nowadays, when genius is justified by its capacity to set forth something, *anything*, there is sure to be a conflict between the censor and the aesthete.

The censor certainly has the best of the argument, on principle, even if the particular censor is not always judicious in the exercise of his functions. The censor's ground is essentially that what we do not talk about in public ought not to be written or painted for public presentation. This seems to me entirely reasonable. I have only now come to see the justification of the censor for whom I have always had a sneaking sympathy, although by my status as an outlying member of Bohemia, I have felt obliged to consider him as pernicious. What is pernicious is not the censor, but the ideas which currently control the relations of men. The very conditions that make the artist the lop-sided, crude, uncivilised, person that he usually is, justify the censor to suppress him. They are two rotten apples out of the same basket. And that basket is the world in which we live, the so-called civilisation which wrecks society on the rock of the individual, and wrecks the individual on the rock of his enforced self-defence. Intelligence is held in leash so that we may be able to impose on others, because fullness of knowledge in the world, as on the stock exchange, would equalise opportunities. As long as selves are looked upon as *I*'s and not as objective things, which may, and of right ought to be, known, so long will barbarism and not civilisation be the character of society, and for so long will intelligence be outlawed.

A civilised community is one where thinking, telling, and acting the truth as one conceives it, will not redound to one's disadvantage. If that much is secured, all the rest will be added thereunto.

XXI. Reality

IN EARLIER CHAPTERS I said that both aesthetics and science as knowledge forms were abstractions, and I considered in some detail the nature of the abstractions that were made. In this chapter the argument will have to be carried to a conclusion, and something will have to be said about that from which the abstractions are made. This whole we can call reality, even though there is not intended to be any suggestion of a reality that is metaphysically demonstrated. I have no confidence in such demonstrations and have nothing to do with them. The only reality that I am concerned with is the very empirical one in which our experience falls. And the only important reason for dragging that into a discussion of aesthetics is because it is so often held that aesthetic experience has some very special connection with reality. For this belief I can see no grounds. The position of aesthetics in empirical reality must therefore be considered, and once entered upon, reality will inevitably lead to some further remarks.

It is hardly necessary today to insist that science deals with abstractions, that it is not an adequate account of existences, but that we can only believe that the world is such that scientific explanation applies to it. Science is not a falsification, except for those who believe that it pretends to far more than any adequate exponent would claim for it. For aesthetics, on the other hand, extravagant claims are not uncommon. Science is so definite in its statements that the limitations of its scope can be intelligibly determined, but the same thing is not true for aesthetics. Its expressions have no clear frontiers; they are organic in quality; they seem extensible enough to include infinity and all lesser things, as items within the field of their actual contacts.

I can see no evidence whatever that aesthetic expression has such a realistic quality. I think that the belief in this property of it is due to the habitual absurdity of taking some kind of aesthetic experience which is richer than others to have a different degree of essential validity. It is like the supposition that the big trees of California are more essentially trees than the little trees elsewhere. If an objective test were possible it might be shown that different aesthetic experiences have reference to different grades of fact. But the uniqueness of the aesthetic fact which has been sufficiently dwelt on, the absence in it of any reference to something else, makes impossible any other test than its inherent quality. It is true that in some cases of aesthetic experience we seem to touch the poles of being, but there is no evidence that when we feel that way we are really touching anything out of the usual. We may have that enormous feeling, possibly, only because the object of our interest has an unusually rich completeness.

Any felt poise has the same fundamental quality of expansive reality, that any other has. If we stand quietly with outstretched arms, breathing calmly and regularly, while emptying our minds of definite content, we will soon come to a sort of felt balance which gradually grows more expansive and comprehensive. In that condition we are, so far as intrinsic evidence goes, as near to a contact with reality as we will ever get. We feel ourselves in a very whole sort of way. As an aesthetic object the whole of that experience is of quite the lowest sort, for it has no internal structure and belongs to the kind that has place and individual quality, but neither direction nor interval. It is typical of the felt wholes of mystic experience in general, and in actual practice that kind of poise is the commonest road to the full-developed mystic orgy. Aesthetically speaking its product is always of a very low grade, however rich it may be in other ways. As I cannot regard feeling as anything other than a vague knowing, I cannot look on the felt thing as given in a more real sense, though of course it may be, and often is, given in a more inclusive one, than when the knowing is distinct.

The aesthetic object is, for me, given through feeling, and it can therefore have no more validity in respect of its self-existent character than the feelings from which it derives. It is a commonplace that feeling is extraordinarily perceptive, and equally fallible. Authors, like common people, like to talk about the infallible intuition of women, and ignore the fact that a large proportion of the crooks and confidence men in the world make their living off this intuition. Two women will have contradictory intuitions, and each will be sure that hers is the authentic one. I have more than once been approached by evangelists who told me that of course they could see that I was an educated man and had read a lot of books, no doubt, while they were only humble simple people, but—Often I pointed out to them that others with very different doctrines had said the same kind of thing to me, *but* that never seemed to impress them in the least. They could always see the quite peculiar authenticity of their own revelations, and needed nothing more in the way of proof. The Catholic Church, which, like all other institutions, is selectively naïve, has limited naïvety to the infallibility of popes and councils. For particular persons it makes rigorous inquisition, to know whether their intuitions are of God or the Devil.

The aesthetic intuition is on all fours with the other kinds. It gives us an impression of the real because there is no other proof of its validity than its general plausibility, which in any particular instance is judged by some individual sentiment or by a consensus of impression. This has inevitably something of quite fantastic idiosyncrasy, and in the last analysis, authenticates everything. If the aesthetic makes a contact with reality in some peculiar sense, then every aesthetic experience has this kind of value. As soon as one makes discriminations, one destroys one's foundations.

The only basic reason one can have for the belief that reality and aesthetics are closely connected, and that one is a means for knowing the other, is the assurance that feeling in man is continuous with feeling in general, and that feeling is in some way the stuff of which the world is made. This supposes that feeling feels itself, just as the ultra-rationalists suppose that mind knows itself. So far as anything can be intelligible about these two attitudes in their ultimate interpretation, they come to about the same thing. In the one case you come to the Absolute mind which somehow involves everything, and in the other case you come to an equally Absolute feeling. Neither side of the controversy has ever very much to say for itself, therefore it spends itself chiefly in disproving the other fellow. One almost always reads in reviews of philosophical books that the critical part is well done but that the constructive part is not successful. This is natural. All philosophers disagree with all others, and they are not usually too critical of the stick with which other critics belabour the common enemy. But the same man who as critic was an accomplice in demolishing a third party, becomes an enemy as soon as one wants to put over the product of one's own factory. Therefore it is more satisfactory to oneself to be critical rather than to be constructive, since one does to a certain measure include in oneself a critic of oneself, and one has, if there is no essentially religious conviction at the back of one's own criticism than in one's own constructions. Consequently it happens so often in the ultra-critical modern period, that a philosopher will have published quantities of criticism and die with his system still unborn, or have it brought to a late though somewhat premature birth because he is invited to give some Gifford lectures or others.

Of late years Bergson has given to feeling an encouraging uplift. Philosophers have for ages tried to apply to the world as a whole the logic of science, but the attempt has always failed. It implied that the network of abstractions could cover the field so completely that nothing could escape the meshes. But one thing always escaped, and that was the puzzling fact that new things happened which could be registered and about which another extension of the net could be thrown. But as this sort of thing was happening all the time, and as the net could not be completed beforehand, the philosopher who would a scientist be, was always lagging behind. Bergson threw aside the logic of science, and substituted the logic of feeling. The difficulty was to find any such thing. He made it up out of instincts, but the feeling doesn't work.

The instinct of an atom, if the atom has any, is infallible. Of course I mean atom in the literal sense of the ultimate datum of science, to which something in the real world may or may not correspond. It is infallible because an atom is not an organism, and therefore it is always in the right place. A tennis ball is in the right place for the driver when his opponent cannot return it, but it is in the wrong place for the opponent. The ball itself is, however, impartial so far as the players are concerned. Even if it were organic and had a memory, it would, like the hedge-hogs that served as croquet-balls for Alice and the Queen of Hearts, be unconcerned about the game. That is not a part of its integral system.

Instincts and feelings imply a relevant system. For instance, the carrion fly lays its eggs on meat, often on rotten meat. It is said at times to lay them on the skunk cabbage or some other foul-smelling plants where the grub will not be able to find nourishment. A partial stimulus, the smell, leads to a discharge of an organic response for which it pulls the trigger. If the feeling is only like some kind of inadequate knowledge which cannot discriminate very clearly, the mistake of the fly, the imperfection of its adjustment to something that smells right but is otherwise wrong, will be explained. But if as Bergson holds there is some kind of *sympathy* at work which is more than this, if feeling makes connection otherwise than through the usual psycho-physical connections, mistakes like this ought not to occur. If instinct works like a combination of purely physical response and a low order of knowledge—and the frequent blunders of instinct due to a response to a partial stimulus seem to indicate this—then there is no reason for supposing that feeling has anything peculiar in its nature. It is not a peculiar sympathy, and gives us no special kind of responses. It is, of course, possible to turn to very mysterious instincts like the homing of birds and others, but to do so is illegitimate. Simple cases of anything may be taken as fair samples of the kind of thing, if it is really that kind of thing that one is talking about. If it is some other kind of thing, then the case is different. Ordinary instinctive processes are not demonstrably different from knowing. In both there is a condition in the organism leading to change, and there are stimuli leading to a response, which serves to discharge the organic functions more completely. The one process of knowing is more adequate in some ways, and the other in some other ways. Neither completely excludes the other nor does it give, so far as there is any clear evidence, a world that is to the other unknown.

It is only atoms that form a perfect society. The world of atoms is a perfectly dependable one. The inorganic world is very much like it unless memory should in some form enter the crystalline world, and cause reactions to be modified by what has no objective present reference. But as soon as erring organisms happen, and the illustration that I have taken from the carrion fly might have been taken from much simpler ones, perhaps even from the simplest, the native harmony of existence is upset, and things are started on the road to knowledge. Sympathy could be perfect among atoms, but once we leave them we have, I think, the best grounds for believing that it will never again be found except in the perfect society which I have tried to point toward, in what I said of objective selves.

The methods of science and aesthetics, which are the two cognitive modes, become distinct when knowing is explicit, but both are involved in less developed forms. Recognition is perhaps the most elementary of these. Below this lies a precognitive form which is given by use, and extended by analogy. This range constitutes the ground of recognition. In this we have the basic conditions where discovery can go on, where things are taken to be what they seem to be either in use or in analogy, where the law of contradiction bothers no one, and where cause is as obvious as the presence of anything in particular. It is only when aesthetic and scientific knowledge part from each other, when fact and truth cease to be identical, that trouble comes and myth-making ceases to be sufficient. We then come to the antinomies, these bugbears of the philosopher, the one and the many, motion and rest, time and eternity, freedom and determinism—all the abysses and terrors that are hidden in the three little words—A, IF, AND,—A, the question of the individual; IF, the question of possibility and choice; AND, the question of multiplicity, of the one and the many. These are the "flowers in the crannied wall" of philosophy, and anyone who could tell what they mean for all purposes, and not only for those of mathematical science, could "tell what God and man is."

Neither aesthetics or science can successfully invade each other's territory, and there exists no form of knowledge which bridges the gap or includes them both. Aesthetic knowing leaves atomic knowledge in the rudimentary stage of mere recognition. Things are sufficiently known to hold their places in aesthetic wholes. They are recognised and put to service under an alien master. Scientific knowledge so stresses the part in relations, that it is acquainted with wholes only as the result of discovery. When the discovery is made, the whole is taken up as an element in relations, and its personal identity is at once abandoned. Science and aesthetics are not enemies. They eat out of the same dish, but their digestive systems are different, and they assimilate in very different ways the nutriment that they have taken.

The only whole that man can know is the whole of practice, but this is a transitive whole, the whole of the passing moments, and he can never get this into his power comprehensively, and at once, but he must live it as it passes. It is the whole of the successive events by which he is made, and which he in turn helps to make, like other creatures. The whole world is instrumental to every creature in it in so far as it affects him, and in this respect man is no different from the rest. His distinction is that he can create instruments which are permanent, which endure, and which are instrumental only for the mind that makes them. All other instruments can be set to work, but knowledge cannot. It must come back to the source from which it sprang. Man can use knowledge only on himself and only indirectly on other things.

Knowledge can make more knowledge, and it can make man equal in effectiveness to the extent of the potentialities of the knowledge, but it can make him great only in that respect. It does not give him new faculties, but only higher potencies of the old. The antinomies remain incomprehensible, for they arise in practice which is saltatory, which permits as much skipping from one thing to another as is consistent with *practicable* continuity. But science and aesthetics are not satisfied with this loose sort of continuity. Each wants its kind of continuity as perfect as possible, and every breach is a defect. Science must assimilate discovery, the introduction of novelties, as well as it can. Aesthetics has to put up with the fact that it must use materials to get its unities. Each type of knowledge converts the hoppety-skippety facts of practice according to its needs, and in so doing ignores an important part of what practice offers. Philosophy is a pseudo-knowledge which attempts to add a dimension to human capacity. It operates in this way because man would like to know things, even if he sees no real way of doing it. Philosophy is science without verification, mixed up with aesthetics that purports to go beyond fact and assert truth. Therefore it always involves a little prestidigitation, or some white magic.

Twenty-five years ago, when I tried to find out rather resolutely what "identity" meant, I discovered, or thought that I did, that it meant nothing more than the possibility of substitution in a given context. For example, if a man is very hungry, any kind of food is the same for him as any other. He makes no distinction except its capacity to satisfy hunger. If he is only moderately hungry he will eat one thing with relish and another thing indifferently. The identity in the context of a famishing state, does not hold for a condition of lessened desire. The same sort of thing can be applied to propositions or situations of all degrees of abstractness.

After I had thought of this, I wondered whether my pre-existing inability to read philosophy had not been due to the fact that all the philosophers who solved the great problems did, at some point or other, cross the abyss between science and aesthetics by means of the bridge which in some oriental religions is named OM. This word expresses an ineffable fact. To pronounce it is productive of great results, provided one has the faith to perceive them. In reading philosophy I had been so often held up by something that seemed so remarkably like the great word OM, that it seemed to me worthwhile trying on it the particular interpretation suggested by the law of the context. It worked beautifully. Bradley and Royce, on whom I first tried this, and of whose works I had never been able to understand anything, became quite simple when one noted that they used the law of the context or ignored it according to their convenience. By using it they discouraged others who sought apparently intelligible solutions, and by ignoring it they attained to their own absolute ones. Before this time I could not read philosophy because I tried to understand it. Since then I can read it with great pleasure, but I leave the understanding of it to the authors who made it. OM is an essential link in every complete philosophical chain, and since no chain is stronger than its weakest link, this link deprives philosophy of every claim to be truly a kind of knowledge.

If to philosophy is denied any real adequacy, and if aesthetics is not the knowledge of any peculiar *real*, we must be content to know what we can by using our intelligence as fully as possible, within the limitations of science and aesthetics. It is always possible to go wrong, and often it is easy. It often seems preferable, and it is only by an extension of the field that must be counted in, that apparently preferable error is proved to be undesirable. We have come to know that disinterested scientific work is alone capable of giving the range of view that enables science to become a basis for far-reaching and important changes in our ways, but we have not yet come to see that aesthetics is of any particular importance. Its only character that has been taken seriously, its capacity for producing emotional stimulation, is adapted specially to a self that is trivial like the aesthetic self, or to one that is sick and needs either a stimulus to make it well, or a toy to make it forget its troubles.

Emotional response, in so far as it becomes a cause of satisfaction, is practical. There is no evidence that one kind is intrinsically better than another. None the less the superior person belabours the inferior one for indulging the wrong emotion, or the right emotion on the wrong occasion. He has, of course, no evidence that his emotion is rightly indulged, except the assurance of his superiority. He says that he is right, and that the other man is wrong, and as he makes more or less a business of this sort of thing, his claim is allowed by the plain man who, unless he is a collector or is shocked by something that he considers indecent, doesn't really care very much.

Let us suppose, however, that pure aesthetic experience exists, and that we become really interested in the world of aspects; that we become habituated to beauty as much, at least, as we have become habituated to cleanliness; that we dislike ugliness and incoherence as we dislike bad smells. The conditions to be taken into account are obviously much more varied and complex than they are for cleanliness. They will depend on a much greater variety of knowing. To take one instance only—speech. Flatness, smartness—except as a sauce—imprecision, rubber-stamps, inflated verbiage, and a hundred other horrors, would become objectionable. People who use words with precision need accuracy of knowledge. The aesthetic symbol would get a new lease of life because it would be subjected to a criticism from our experience generally, and would be sensitively related to truth. For a trifling example take what Livingstone said of lions—that they were not brave but cowardly. If this were true and generally known, it would turn the phrase lion-hearted into a mere verbal symbol, or lead to its disuse. This is the sort of thing that does happen in good poetry. The language is kept fresh by being related to such knowledge as the poet possesses. It is a direction that offers a large range either for romantic exuberance or classic restraint. It is a way of making and keeping language civilised.

I give this instance of language because it is an obviously relevant one. Of course the same kind of thing applies almost everywhere. It would have very little meaning for one whose notion of aesthetic interest is the occasional reading of a book or looking at a picture. But its meaning might be very different for one who found our present civilisation to be something appalling with its fragmentary strenuousness, its discouraging successes, and its disheartening failures. To such a one there might be a gain if there could be an interest in a world, in a society, which was really presentable, which one would care to keep wholly in view. This picture could not of itself be evidence of validity. Aesthetics gives us fact, not truth. But fact to be interesting to adults in the long run, must be true. Only science and practice can judge validity beyond the mere aspect. The world as it is scientifically known is not a whole world, but the nature of that world is such that it can find in science a partial reflection that is true enough to work. Our aesthetic perception of the world must not contradict this knowledge. It need include no more than is relevant, but the persistent attempt to make fact and truth concordant is the basis of an aesthetic interest that can go beyond "aestheticism," without becoming applied aesthetics.

The competent spectator would under those circumstances not be a person who is conversant with masterpieces and the lore of museums, but a man whose interest was wide, whose self was unified, and whose mind and body were active. No result for such a man would be final except as it went into the making of a social picture that he would like to contemplate. I do not mean to imply anything so foolish as that he would be always thinking of this end, or explicitly aiming at it. I refer to something like the service of God among the truly pious. There is a larger end of interest, which is also partly revealed in pictures of detail. A world which one can both believe in—the world of science, and look at—the world of aesthetics, is the end to be desired.

There is no profit for such an end in believing what one knows is not true. To the simple-minded person this statement might seem foolishly unnecessary, since it would seem to him obvious that one cannot believe a thing which one knows is not true. If this were really impossible there would be no neurotics, there would be no good party-men except morons, there would be no hundred-percenters of any kind. All these people, and all others, to some extent keep different and incompatible books of their beliefs. So long as society is not co-operative but is competitive, and consequently we have to fight for our *self*-preservation, we shall have to keep these double and triple series of books, one for the things as they affect *us* (which of course includes those in whom we are interested), one for the things as they affect those who oppose *us*, and another for the things that we can see without being distorted either by self-defence or attack. A genuine inability to believe the things that one knows are not true, would bring about the greatest revolution that society has ever known. That change will mark the dawn of civilisation.

It remains now only to show the relation of pure science and pure aesthetics to practice in the largest sense. Science and aesthetics are incidents in the comprehensive practical world. Practice means change. Only that which is not practical can endure. What thus endures is knowledge which man projects in the course of his practical living. But this knowledge, which is given in successive stages as just what it is, returns into the life of the men that make it to help in their transformation. Knowledge which is really assimilated means a change in the knower. Most of our knowledge, however, which is not a knowledge of manufacturing processes in one sense or another, is so conventional, so merely schematic, so confused, and so little assimilated or else assimilated with so little of clear direction, that it leaves us almost as we were, or sends us off at random tangents. People have commonly noted and often with dismay, how little they learn from experience. They repeat the same blunders, commit the same offences, tumble into the same holes over and over again, although they know it all so well. Popular expressions abound to illustrate this. Hell's pavement of good intentions, and New Year's resolutions, are instances in point. My own redirection in life came when I posed to myself the definite question—How can one learn by experience? The way of conceiving aesthetics, and many other things, that I have set forth in this book, is the result of the answer that I found.

I said that most of our knowledge leaves us just as we were. To some extent this is reasonable when we have been concerned with science, since in science the relation of the self is reduced to low terms of particularity. The self for science is the self that can perceive external relations, and keeps its other individualities in the background. The application of science to the individual is indirectly made through the invention of instruments. This apart from the influence of the attitude of truth-seeking which might, but does not always, directly affect his nature. But in aesthetics the knower's feeling self, with its rich inner relations and its wide range of outer approaches to things, is implicated. Every such experience which is freshly had may have the effect of modifying that feeling self, thereby modifying the pictorial interest, and the quality of the man that makes it. The real goal would be attained if in science a man was ready to perceive all truth impartially, and if in aesthetics a man's acceptance of a "picture" and his enjoyment became identical.

I have said little about enjoyment except to dismiss it from pure aesthetics entirely, and to give it a place only as applied aesthetics. To the serious artist enjoyment is the same as the realisation of a creative interest. He enjoys a picture when he has made it, just as he enjoys food when he is hungry. He does, in fact, hunger for that completed achievement as the virtuously-inclined hunger after righteousness. Other enjoyments he may have, but they are either little things like the licking of one's lips or the patting of one's tummy after a good meal; or else they are the satisfactions of his self-feelings, which are related to the pure aesthetic ones as the saint's self-satisfaction in getting to heaven is related to the contemplation of the radiant Godhead.

If aesthetics could be recognised as the important thing that it would be in a world that was resolutely intelligent, that refused to subordinate almost everything to a possessive interest whose magnificent consequence is conspicuous expenditure—if pure aesthetics could find a place—there would be little or no difference between knowing and enjoying. The essential attitudes would be those of making, and of accepting or rejecting. All fresh seeing is creative, and that is acceptable which fulfils a need. The interest in objects, taken objectively and not possessively, intensifies the need and cultivates it. Experience would become more commonly creative because the interests of the self would enforce and not destroy the authentic character of objects. At present it is more important that a thing should be *mine* than that it should *be*. The property interest in beautiful things begins to be most active when the creative interest is ended. The field of this creative interest is conventionally limited, whereas the essential value of it would depend upon the unrestricted use and extension. This extension of range depends on the right relation of possession and use. The tendency of a complex culture is to stimulate activity. The tendency of anything that could in a eulogistic sense be called civilisation, is to stimulate creativeness which is profoundly and vitally different from, and opposed to, possessiveness. Creation is the perfect condition of use, but all the things that I have spoken of as applied aesthetics are minor legitimate forms. Many of them are overdeveloped in a society which is pathological, because of its infantile fixations. It is a commonplace that our moral culture has not kept pace with our science, which is another way of saying the same thing. It means that our moral and social attitudes are primitive and barbarous, and that they have not assimilated our science.

The crux of the matter lies in the self. Unless we can get to the point of seeing that selves are not *we* but only *us*, that we defend the past at the expense of the future, that we defend our possessions at the expense of the future, that we defend our possessions at the expense of creative effort, and that we defend our mistakes at the cost of corrected replacements—unless we can take all knowledge to be freely our province, progress will be only the pendulum swing from one excess to another. True balance can be found only in a freedom which permits of knowing all and taking the consequence. To repeat, civilisation is the character of a social state where the individual is free to think, speak, act, as truly as he likes without suffering harm thereby. In that way only can we reach out beyond brutality or sentimentalism to a world where ideals are the self-projections of progressing knowledge, and not the attempts of pathological visionaries to remedy what they do not understand.

XXII. Art

THE DISTINCTION BETWEEN THE fine art and the others, should not, in my opinion, have currency. It is a social convention, and like all social conventions causes confusion when it is taken for something else. It is incapable of definition except when we leave aside so many of the facts that the definition becomes a mere play of words. A tool handle is often as beautiful as a piece of sculpture, not because it is looked at as though it were sculpture, but because of its fascinating adaptation to the hand. Sculpture is, however, often directly interesting and satisfying because the planes have this tactile attractiveness, even if they are only looked at. Neither for that matter do I have to handle the axe or plane, or whatever it may be, in order to realise its quality. But the tool handle was not given that precise quality for any other reason than that it is therefore useful. The same thing is true of much painting and sculpture. The development of the planes was the result of a desire to make the picture a lifelike and enduringly interesting record of a person, a scene, or an event. Some works of art are intended uniquely to satisfy an aesthetic self, but if we take art production on the whole, now and in the past, we shall certainly find that they are the exception. The notion of the fine art is a result of an attempt to account for a few peoples' reactions on exceptional occasions, and it takes but little note of what happens to most people whether producers or contemplators, most of the time. It is futile and useless.

It is much better to call everything art which is deliberately produced by man, and not to be too fussy about the deliberation. Within that whole, innumerable classifications can be made for all sorts of passing reasons, but it is best to avoid any that seem to stamp the objects with too definite a character. Definitions are terrible things to inflict on innocent objects, which often have great difficulty in outliving them. Aristotle once defined a tragedy. Nobody has understood the definition, but lots of people during three centuries were held up by it, and spent unbelievable time and energy in trying to show that tragedy was just what Aristotle had pronounced it to be. Such definitions are not illuminating at the best, since objects of this sort have no sufficiently definite character to support definition. Defining cannot be carried on at all except on condition that it is made a game, or that one neglects most of the relevant facts.

We commonly think of art as the production of objects that can be shown, but even this limitation of meaning is not practicable. In my own experience there is nothing that is more aesthetically important than seeing pictorially, although this produces nothing that can be shown to another. As I have repeatedly said, the only psychological truth that is of much importance for aesthetics is the active, impulsive character of mental process. Aesthetic vision is not only an active process, but it may become a finely regulated one. Since it is not a condition of having things tumbling into your eyes, but of going out to find them, it is definite creation. The result is art.

That the distinction between a specifically material aesthetic object and a mental one can be rightly obscured, is not in contradiction with common fact. A picture is no more seen by the simple act of turning the eyes upon it than a landscape is. You and I may be looking at a painted canvas on which one sees a picture and the other only paint splotches. The fact that the picture was made by a man, and that the landscape is no more than a bit of countryside which is seen by someone, is much less important than the way in which each is seen. Art can in no case be confined to handwork, and it is difficult to see how any limitations can be placed upon the meaning of the term.

Art is human activity, and it is most vital when it is creative, and not routine or repetitive. Of course routine work is necessary, and repetition is not only useful but it is often pleasant and comforting. Of creative work the highest forms are scientific, aesthetic, and inventive. Invention is the production of novelties in all lines, of which science and aesthetics are the most important, but invention has a field in all the lesser forms of object-making which I described in an earlier chapter. The fine arts have their place in the general class of things made by man, and much is lost while nothing is gained by pretending for them a special character and importance.

Throughout this book I have laid stress on the creation of objects, and have insisted that object-making is man's significant activity, when he has passed beyond the limits of practice in its most restricted sense. It is desirable to stick to this mode of dealing with things and to leave the classification of things themselves to science, whose business it is to make the classifications as accurate as possible. There are no easy classifications in art which are of more than casual use, which are more than passing conveniences. Description of attitudes which define relations of the maker or observer are more practicable, because they tell about modes of action which are somewhat definite, even though flexible, without making any attempt to lessen their flexible adaptability. Attitudes toward particular things change from moment to moment, or remain comparatively fixed for some period of time. When change takes place the object changes, and no descriptive subtlety can define these changes in the object in any useful way. They are infinitely various; they are known as just what they are to the experiencer; and a great deal is lost while nothing is gained by crude attempts at classification. Classifications of that sort are about as accurate and much less useful than classifications of books in a library. The latter enable us to find the books, whereas the former serve chiefly for general conversation and critical disquisitions.

The effect of thinking in terms of Fine Arts is almost altogether bad. It encourages the museum, the dilettante, the collector, the critic, and other futilities of a pseudo-civilisation. Its only good excuse for being is its economic benefits for a certain class of producers. The notion of the fine arts and their putative value encourage conspicuous expenditure, and without this there would be very little occupation for the artist in our current social order. The importance of the *fine arts* is rigorously economic.

One of the worst consequences of the fine-arts notion is the value attached to things that are gathered into museums and collections. Museums are occasionally visited by persons seeking recreation, but more commonly by those who go there on purpose. The purpose is often "culture," whatever that may mean; often it is a felt obligation to "know," which, I suppose, means to become acquainted with, the best that has been done and said in the world; otherwise it is usually a desire to learn the history of art.

It is very difficult to understand just what a history of art is. There is, of course, a proper subject for history in technical methods, but this cannot be studied except by specialists. There can be histories of special motives or of formal characters, but these are obviously of interest only to a limited class of students. What is commonly called the history of art is a meaningless mixture of dates, biographical facts, art criticism, and general history. Art is one of the incidental items of human behaviour. It is a part of general history. But when it is so taken it has no independent continuity, which can be abstracted from the whole and given a separate treatment. Especially, it cannot be mixed up with art criticism. Shakespeare as a particular person was a man who lived from 1564 to 1616, doing certain things, and related to the life of the time in certain ways. What Shakespeare was to the eighteenth century is part of eighteenth-century history. What Shakespeare is to us is part of our history, but the usual historical way of treating an artist in terms of the writer's present interest, applied to the time when that artist lived, is absurd. Art history is almost never history; it is not aesthetic criticism, which cannot be historical; it is an utterly unilluminating hodge-podge and a misleading waste of time. In general histories, art is usually gathered into special chapters and treated in a similar fashion, instead of entering into the current of the narrative in so far as it is a factor in the history that is the subject matter of the book. Art as a more special subject is a part of the history of social life, wherein political and economic matter enters in the same incidental and explanatory way, that social life including art, enters into political and economic history. Histories of fine art are quite useless and teach next to nothing of history which they only deform, and very little of art.

Of the dilettante I have spoken already in connection with the aesthetic self. The dilettante plays an aesthetic game. He makes implicit or explicit rules for what is to count and what is not to count. His rules change with the aesthetic fashions, indeed without fashions the life of the aesthete would be a bore. A change in aesthetic fashion gives him a new lease of life and permits him to start all over again with a new set of interests and standards.

Standards recur once more. They also belong to aestheticism unless they are to belong to ethics. In the latter case they belong to the set of conceptions that lead one to make rules for the future as though prescriptions could outrun knowledge. "Of course we don't know everything but we *do* know that ... ." *That* often proves to be the thing which precisely we do not know.

For aestheticism standards are useful, since every game must have its rules. People often say to me on occasion of talk about this painter or that, "But how about Cézanne?" I can only answer with one convenient set of words or another—"Damn Cézanne." There was a moment when Cézanne brought me something fresh which I assimilated with great enthusiasm and joy. What Cézanne gave was important, but his own expression of it was limited, constrained, and in many ways extremely insufficient, and when I had made the assimilation I found very little of him left over that is endurable. For a while, no painter excited my interest more vitally. Now no pictures interest me less. He is for me more completely the squeezed lemon than any other artist of anything like equal importance.

The aesthete can only with difficulty understand my attitude. He can understand the acceptance of Cézanne or his rejection, but Cézanne as a serviceable episode is unintelligible. Several times people of this sort who have never seen anything in Cézanne tell me that they are glad to find that I have come round to their views. It is useless to tell them that I have not, that I don't own any views in their sense of the word, because my language is utterly meaningless to them. They believe that there is something right or wrong in the matter, that there are objective judgments, and that their latest judgments have this valuable property in the highest degree. Why their judgments rather than those of other people or of other times should be so distinguished, I have never been able to find out. Their attitude of conviction, like that of many others, is a subject for psychopathology, and has very little interest apart from that.

Standards naturally lead to *critics*. Perhaps the worse consequence of the fine-arts notion is the critical function. The connoisseur is called in German a *Feinschmecker*, a fine-taster, and the fine-taster goes very well with the fine arts. The notion of the fine-arts critic as contrasted with the technical critic is that the latter is a judge of something by virtue of its action on something else, while the former is a judge of it by virtue of its action on him. Since he cannot be submitted to any test of competence, his judgments are preferences, and nothing more. Preferences are grounds of judgment only when there are no other consequences. From the fine arts there are none, therefore they are the special field of glory for the critic. He spangles and sputters all over the place. He helps people to appreciate and to depreciate. So he has a social function. He helps prices to do the same thing, and so he has an economic function. In more reputable lines of trade this is done by advertisers whose purposes cannot be open to question. Critics range through the whole scale from those who will tell the truth that they believe, or that they are committed to, though the heavens fall, to those who differ from advertisers merely in name. My own sympathy is with the latter, though I wish that they would change the name.

There is something curious in this matter of criticism. In most trades it is not considered either good form or legally permissible to denigrate the goods of another. There is a responsibility for public statements. But making works of fine art is apparently not a business, a trade, or a profession. The man who makes a living by them is subjected to all the inconveniences that would result if it were one or another of these things, but he enjoys a preferential treatment of abuse. Critics loose their arrows very much at random against the men who are struggling for life, using not only their own very inadequate powers of judgment, but irrelevant standards of accomplishment besides. Whether they do this to protect the public or simply to utter themselves, I do not know. I do know that the better class of critic is often the most unjust, because he has a reputation to keep up, and there is less repercussion from a failure to recognise a great man, than there is from a mistaken over-estimate of a little one. It is damning to be held up as the person who took X to be the great painter of our time. Therefore the critics whose morals are most above reproach are more undesirable than those whose object is to boom their class of goods, and who proclaim as many masterpieces as possible.

The critic—I am of course not here concerned with the critic who is an historian, a literary artist, or a sort of quasi-scientific analyst—has rather an absurd position. He seems to be a sort of protector of public morals. It is his business to see that artists do not prostitute their talents, that their integrity should be maintained. Why the least important class in the community should be held to the highest standard of conduct, I do not know. Of course without the fiction of the fine arts no such demand could possibly be made. Some fantastic psycho-analyst might hold that in this way society compensates for its profound immorality, demanding that a true picture should be held up before it, so that it might know its real face even if it does not heed the warning. It is more likely that there is a traditional connection between the artist and the priest, and the artist and the magician, a connection with that which exhorts, prophesies, and remakes life. The basis is essentially superstitious, and outworn. It is sheer fatuity to hold the artist to any other standard of integrity than that of the community in general, to make the artist an ineffectual symbol of the virtues that society refuses to practise.

Another consequence of the fine-arts notion is the insatiable appetite that people have for absorbing it. If they never looked at a picture or read a poem except when they hunger for it, they would be better off. As it is, I often wonder what they actually do see. When I look at people in a picture gallery pass from one picture to another and see thirty of them in less time than I who am rather experienced can see one, I am forced to believe that they can do little more than be aware that they have seen them. Of course they get an occasional impression when the picture is sufficiently reminiscent, or is sufficiently obvious, but they can see nothing fresh—to be paradoxical—until it has become stale. In the main, however, they have found some more subjects for conversation, and they can express opinions about the latest thing, which is, with other things as they are, as profitable as to have *seen* it.

We cannot get along without the notion of the fine arts as long as our social conceptions continue to be what they are. As long as ugliness prevails generally and the community follows a way of life that compels it to ignore the obvious and to conceal the evident, as long as truth must be told with such discretion as to become virtual falsehood unless its utterance is warranted and neutralised by literary bluster, for so long the fine arts may serve as a side dish, as a tickler for the appetite, or as a dessert when the appetite is sated. If we ever become radically and not trivially serious, we shall drop the fine arts and take beauty into our lives. Intelligence demands beauty, but it must be an intelligence that has the courage to see things through.

THE END